"Mom, I love this book! It does
it is a good heartfelt read!"
~ Isabe
Age 9

"Brought comfort to my heart and tears to my eyes.
Thank you yet again!!!" (What's It Like Dad?)
~ Vandy Winker Palazzo

"Awww ... I loved this story!!! It must go into the book!!!"
(Godiva Chocolates and the Honeymoon)
~ Anna Bongiovanni

"You really do worm your way into our hearts!"
(Don't Let Go!)
~ Sherrie Robbins

"Beautiful ... the tears are flowing." (What's It Like Dad?)
~ Marcia Brown Eugeni

"I needed this story, Bob ... thank you for sharing."
(What's It Like Dad?)
~ Anne Dykstra

"Boy, that really hit me!!! Faith and wonderful memories
keep us going!"(What's It Like Dad?)
~ Maureen C. Mahoney-Vitello

"Brilliant. Absolutely brilliant!" (Telephone Calls - Realtor)
~ Mark Timon

"That is so sweet... and, now, I want pancakes."
(Silver Dollar Pancakes)
~ Peggy McCarthy Jenkins

"I can still hear my daughter yelling the same words ... about 35 years ago ... a very nostalgic story that all fathers can relive in their minds ... great story!" (Don't Let Go!)
~ Larry Schiro

"This was beautiful, most definitely one of my favorites." (What's It Like Dad?)
~ Cindy Ciccarelli

"Beautiful, read it crying but smiling." (What's It Like Dad?)
~ Mary Jordan

"I am so grateful to call you my friend!"
~ Kathy Wade Iodice

"I love everything you write, but this was especially spectacular. You are a master with words and present the story perfectly. It is emotional, meaningful and powerful, and should be required reading in every school in the United States. The message is that important!!!!"
(I Never Knew!)
~ Alan Carrel

"Wow, I feel the tears welling up in my eyes, but then again, a big smile on my face. Feeling beautiful emotions from this tale, so thank you my friend for sharing with all of us."
(What's It Like Dad?)
~ Sandra Fabiano Supon

"Those memories are with us forever ... such gifts!"
(Single Sugar, Double Cream)
~ Ellen Latham

"Dogs ... ahhhh ... God gave us a truly special gift when he gave us dogs. They are such pure and loving souls." (Mia)
~ Kim Devitte

"I wept tears of joy, happiness, and faith. Beautifully inspired, written, & shared. Thank you my friend & counselor." (What's It Like Dad?)

~ Michael Miller-Mercer

"Such a beautiful memory, it brought tears to my eyes. So blessed to have such wonderful dads." (Single Sugar, Double Cream)

~ Cindy Teeto

"Thank you for this wonderful story. It's such a beautiful story of your father ..." (Single Sugar, Double Cream)

~ Eleanor Migliazzo Novara

"You're killing me here Robert, I'm on my fourth beer and while reading your story my eyes are welling up!" (Faith, Family & Baseball)

~ John Pellow, Sr.

"You are a wonderful, fantastic storyteller." (Faith, Family & Baseball)

~ Marie Giordano Campagna

"Oh I love this story, the ending line ... filled with much LOVE" (Don't Let Go!)

~ Toni Manzare

"I love this beautiful story!!!" (631-0865)

~ Rosa Pullano Zito

"Beautiful story of beautiful people and as it should be for you two timeless love birds. Bob, I am a Romantic who's grateful for you sharing this with us." (631-0865)

~ Michael Miller-Mercer

"Wow that really touched my soul, you have such a gift - keep using it." (What's It Like Dad?)
~ Kathy Rubino

"I always enjoy your stories Bob, but this one was the best. What a great way to start my day. And I agree with Alan, you are a wonderful writer." (631-0865)
~ Barbara Nuchereno

"What a beautiful memory of how it began and continues on today. Some things are definitely meant to be, right from the beginning and this reinforces that ... it was meant to be!" (631-0865)
~ Kerrie Keller Piaskowski

"I couldn't stop crying! Ever the most beautiful story!" (What's It Like Dad?)
~ Crystal Garneau

"Love this!!! Great story!! (631-0865)
~ Laurianne Martinez-Griffis

"Robert thank you for the kind and loving words that you have shared about my brother and the friendship you shared. Reading your story has touched my heart and so glad to know that Lewis has not been forgotten. Thank you so much. True friends are so hard to find. God bless you and thank you again." (I Never Knew)
~ Vanessa Scott

"Beautiful story Bob. Might be my favorite." (631-0865)
~ Sally Viverito Dube

"Beautiful girl, beautiful story, beautiful daughter, beautiful life. Love love love it! I'm not crying. Of course I am." (631-0865)
~ Marcia Brown Eugeni

"Beautiful story with a happy ending!" (631-0865)
>~ Steven Vandervelden

"You've brought me to tears. What a beautiful, bittersweet story." (Calling It A Day)
>~ Gayle Miller Kerman

"Bob … I'm speechless. You pitched. Andrew hit it out of the park. Your connection bespeaks the richness that is possible in the human experience … and so seldom achieved." (Calling It A Day)
>~ Mark Timon

"I have no words to adequately describe how this touched my heart. It definitely resonates with me. Moms are incredible." (You Can Still Love)
>~ Colleen Lauer Barone

"So beautifully remembered motherly love. Thank you, my friend!" (You Can Still Love)
>~ Father Marijan Procyk

"Such a beautiful story… reminds me of the age old saying: Don't judge a book by its cover!" (Jesse James and the Lunch Lady)
>~ Susan A. Szczublewski

"Such a beautiful story of a loving mother and her loving son." (You Can Still Love)
>~ Rosa Pullano Zito

"Love this! Simply adorable!" (631-0865)
>~ Donna Mueller

"Beautiful, I felt every word." (Calling It A Day)
>~ Donna Muoio

"Just beautiful Bob. True friendships are color blind."
(I Never Knew)

~ Angela Vicino Mecca

"This is so sweet, love this story." (631-0865)
~ Cindy Ciccarelli

"Once in a great while a student will touch your heart,
as every teacher knows. Your story has love and respect
sprinkled all over it. Beautiful." (Calling It A Day)
~ Jennifer Gallagher

"OMG what a story! I got the chills! Made me feel just like I
was there as usual!" (Thank You Harold Burns)
~ Marcia Brown Eugeni

"Aww ... such a sweet love story!" (631-0865)
~ Carm Giancola Simon

"Through tears I'm trying to comment but am at a loss for
words. The love that flowed through your pen for your
mother was felt in every word. What a gift."
(You Can Still Love)
~ Joy LeBrasseur Evans

"You are such a mensch. So was Lewis." (I Never Knew)
~ Larry Kerman

"OMG!!!! Thank God everything worked out!! There were so
many emotions in this story. It shows how we have to live
every day to the fullest because it can change so quickly."
(Dogs Are Like That!)
~ Anna Bongiovanni

"Bob, I can't begin to tell you how deeply moving I found this recounting of those days over 10 years ago - touching and so full of what it means to be human, to suffer a frightening loss, face it all with courage and be an even more inspiring person to those of us lucky enough to call you our friend. Much Love." (Dogs Are Like That!)
~ Vic Bahl

And Then It Happened...

Tales to Make You Smile, Laugh, Love, and Remember

By Robert P. Simpson

Illustrations by Frank A. Mariani

www.bumblebeesanddandelions.com

Rights and Permissions: rsimpson@bumblebeesanddandelions.com

Publisher: Robert P. Simpson

Cover Art and Illustrations: Frank A. Mariani

Book Designer: Leslie Taylor
Buffalo Creative Group
www.buffalocreativegroup.com

Editor: Ellie Rummell

Copy Editor: Adelina Simpson, Esq.

Publisher's Cataloging-in-Publication Data

Names:	Simpson, Robert P., author. | Mariani, Frank A., illustrator.
Title:	And Then It Happened ... Tales to make you smile, laugh, love and remember / by Robert P. Simpson; illustrations by Frank A. Mariani.
Description:	Buffalo, New York: Robert P. Simpson [2024]
Identifiers:	ISBN: 979-8-218-37495-2 (hardcover) | 979-8-218-37552-2 (paperback) | 979-8-218-37557-7 (ebook)
Subjects:	LCSH: Coming of age--New York (State)--Niagara Falls. | Storytellers--Biography. | Nostalgia. | Children. | Adulthood. | Middle age. | Love. | Family. | Friendship. | Humorous stories, American. | Short stories, American. | LCGFT: Humor. | Short stories. | BISAC: BIOGRAPHY & AUTOBIOGRAPHY / Personal Memoirs. | HUMOR / Topic / Cultural, Ethnic & Regional.
Classification:	LCC: PS3619.I56395 B86 2024 | DDC: 813.6--dc23

Printed in the United States of America

Dedication

This work is dedicated to my late sister, Mary Louise Peret. Unassuming, talented, kind, caring, loving, generous and a brilliant writer, she is loved and missed beyond measure. Despite her health struggles later in life, she never complained, always smiled, always laughed and always ended every telephone call with, "I love you Bob!" I love you too Mary Lou!

Table of Contents

Acknowledgements

I never would have written these stories without the encouragement of my friends. I love you all! I extend a special thank you to all my Facebook friends who took the time to read and leave a heart, a "like" or a sweet comment. Without those reactions and comments I never would have written these tales.

Once again, the very talented artist, Frank Mariani, has worked his magic to illustrate these stories. Frank has a special gift of being able to listen to an idea or read a few words of my text and then draw exactly what was heretofore only in my mind's eye. He makes my stories come alive as only he can. Thank you, Frank!

Many thanks, also, to Leslie Taylor of Buffalo Creative Group for her excellent work on the book design.

And a special callout to Avi at Rockstars - Creative Agency of Miami, Florida for brilliantly bringing the Blue, Silver and Gold Buttons to life in "The Gold Button", and for his recreation of old newspaper accounts in "What a Jump George!" and "Thank You Harold Burns".

I want to thank Angela Mecca and Sandy Supon, dear friends since our early school days, for reviewing many of my stories before I showed them to anyone else. Thank you also to Angela and Donna Muoio for producing the launch and storytelling event for *And Then It Happened...* Finally, I want to thank my close friend, Marcia Brown Eugeni, for sending me texts and emails encouraging me to write this book. If you think there are too many stories, it is Marcia's fault! She asked me to include them!

And then it happened . . .

Foreword

When my dear friend, Bob Simpson, asked me if I would write the foreword to "And Then It Happened …", I felt greatly honored that he'd bestow such a privilege upon me. Truthfully, I also felt a bit nervous about the prospect of writing a foreword for a book of stories and vignettes by so wonderful a writer and storyteller as Robert Simpson. Because what awaits you, Dear Reader, are remembrances, the stirring of memories that will surely make you, as they did me – smile, as you, too, recall navigating the corridors of both adolescence and high school, laugh in recognition of our common human foibles, and find more than a few lumps in your throat, and tears in your eye when remembering those most dear to us. And, I believe, all the while, they will fill your heart with hope and joy.

It has been said that it is not difficult to notice when an author has love for the characters that inhabit the stories they write. In "And Then It Happened …", there are stories of love in all its forms – the love of a parent for a child, a child's love for a parent, the love that deep friendships bring, love for those that teach and mentor, and even love for those that are strangers to us.

Who can't be moved by the deeply stirring and exquisite tribute to a mother in "You Can Still Love!", or the homage to a remarkable man and father told with humor and wisdom in "Single Sugar, Double Cream". Or the lovingly poetic celebration of love for your Life's Love in "How I Love You". And, when it comes our turn to enjoy the gift of being a parent, the love that can hardly be contained in our heart, brimming over, as is beautifully told in "Happy Birthday, Adelina" and "Don't Let Go!"

We are all susceptible to being misled, and to making quick judgments based on surface appearances – perhaps even more so as adults than as young children. In the stories, "I Never Knew", very touchingly, and in "Jesse James and the Lunch Lady", with wonderful humor, we see these superficialities needn't matter, and that initial judgments can be quite mistaken. These powerful stories serve as a wonderful reminder to us older folks about keeping open hearts and open minds.

There are so many more that I could tell you about, but I'll save for you the joy in their reading, along with the smiles, the laughs, and sometimes tears that these beautiful stories are sure to evoke.

One of my favorite novels, and given its popularity

over these many years, perhaps one of yours as well, is Harper Lee's magnificent "To Kill a Mockingbird". The voice of the character, Scout, who sees the world from the vantage point of an unusually perceptive child, is remarkably moving. In Robert Simpson's "And Then It Happened …", we see a similar perceptive voice sharing its memory.

Harper Lee chose a wonderful, perhaps a bit sardonic quote from the English essayist Charles Lamb as the epigram for her novel: "Lawyers, I suppose, were children once".

Bob Simpson certainly was, and we all should be so very thankful for that.

Vikram Bahl
Amherst, New York
July 18, 2024

Preface

The truth is that I hear these stories in my head. They strike like lightning! I never see them coming. I hear them and envision myself telling them out loud to my friends and family. And, as I am listening, I almost always hear a pause, sometimes two or three, during the course of a tale, where I say, "And then it happened ..."

I only have to write down what I hear. It's as simple as that.

As in my first book, most of these stories are true; the rest are mostly true. I hope you enjoy them. They were all written with love. I hope they bring you a smile, a laugh or inspire a meaningful memory of your own. That is why I write them. And, if any should cause a tear or two, I sincerely hope they are tears of joy.

Smile, laugh, love, and remember!

Robert P. Simpson
Williamsville, New York
July 18, 2024

Happy Birthday Adelina

I didn't know if she heard me, even though I spoke to her every day for months; nine to be exact. She hadn't taken her first breath yet, after all. But it didn't matter – I loved her even then. Love for a child, born or unborn, is like that.

I spoke to her in the morning, sang to her in the afternoon, and softly told her bedtime stories at night. I told her my name, and then I told her hers. I told her she was "Adelina my Ballerina". I told her I loved her mom, and I loved her, and always would.

We prepared for her arrival for months, nine to be precise. I painted her room and assembled her bassinet. Mom bought her pretty clothes and soft blankets and stuffed koala bears. We read parenting books and went to classes for first-time parents. I even took notes.

We rushed to the hospital on February 1. The doctor invited me into the delivery room but warned that I might have to leave if asked. I wouldn't have missed this moment for the world.

Her first sounds were loud and unforgettable, "Wah,

wah, wah, wah, wahhhh!" in a beautiful, thunderous crescendo. She sang this five-word song repeatedly as the nurse carried her to the far side of the room. She sang with all her might as the doctor looked at me and said, "Congratulations – she's a screamer!"

She sang the second verse during foot-printing, "Wah, wah, wah, wah, wahhhh!"

She sang the third verse during a sponge bath, "Wah, wah, wah, wah, wahhhh!"

She sang the fourth verse when the nurse placed her name tag on her tiny ankle. She seemed to like her name, "Adelina Elizabeth" as she sang, "Wah, wah, wah, wah, wahhhh!"

The nurses joined in the chorus, and the anesthesiologist tapped out the beat with his toe. Even the doctor started to hum as my tired wife smiled as only a first-time mom could.

"Wah, wah, wah, wah, wahhhh!" she sang, hanging on that last note.

Swaddling in blankets didn't dim her spirit or quiet her song. She sang the fifth and sixth verses at the top of her lungs as the nurse carried her back across the room and into my open arms. This moment in time will forever be frozen in my memory.

"Wah, wah, wah, wah, wahhhh!" she sang like an angel, happy to be alive, as I held her for the first time.

And then it happened ...

I bowed my head and whispered to her softly, "It's ok Adelina, my Ballerina, daddy's here."

And right then, like magic, her singing stopped, and she started to coo. The room quieted. The nurses and doctors all smiled under their masks and their eyes said what we all knew.

She had heard me after all. She knew my voice. And I loved hers.

Don't Let Go!

I held her in my arms and looked into her eyes and whispered, "I will never drop you – I will always hold you – I will never let go!" She giggled and smiled, safe in daddy's arms. She reached into my shirt breast pocket with her tiny fingers. "Get out of my pocket!" I bellowed. She just laughed and reached deeper. She knew that's where I had hidden a cookie just for her.

Such is the joy of fatherhood. Such is the trusting bond between father and daughter: A promise to always hold her; a promise to never let her fall; a promise to always keep her safe. She was only two then, but time rushed by. Now she was six with new promises to make and new promises to keep.

The church was down the street and around the corner from our house. It had a big parking lot, mostly empty on Saturdays, surrounded by a grassy knoll. We had no sidewalks on our old-time village street, and the neighbors preferred it that way. So kid after kid learned to ride their bikes in the safety of the old church parking lot.

She practiced for weeks on her Disney Princess pink bike with twelve-inch wheels, comforted by a pair of rear-mounted training wheels. Beaming a broad smile from under her shiny new helmet, racing around in circles, she yelled out, "Look at me daddy!" as her confidence grew. There are few things in this world that warm your heart as much as seeing your child learn how to ride a bike.

It was a warm Saturday morning in August when I knew she was ready. My wife had enjoyed many special one-on-one, mother-daughter moments, but this one she gave to me.

"Are you sure?" I asked as I loaded our precious cargo into my minivan.

"You go ahead," she replied, "this one is yours, call me when it's time."

As I drove our six-year-old to the church with tearful eyes, my mind flashed back to Jerauld Avenue and a warm August morning thirty-seven years earlier, when my dad ran up and down the sidewalk behind my blue Schwinn, as I pedaled as hard as I could, and he promised not to let go. I remembered how my dad taught me, and I knew what was coming.

And so it goes ... moms and dads running behind these little bikes ... training wheels removed for the first time ... promising not to let go ... little boys and girls excited and scared at the same time.

She watched with tentative anticipation as I removed

the training wheels in the church parking lot. She was worried. I reassured her.

As she mounted her bike, she looked back at me, making sure I was holding the seat to steady the bike.

"Don't let go, daddy!"

"I won't sweetie!"

"Promise?"

"I promise. Are you ready?"

"Ready!"

I gave her a gentle push and ran behind her, ten feet, twenty feet, thirty feet, in a straight line across the parking lot. She pedaled hard and I ran even harder to keep up. Like thousands of moms and dads before me, I ran behind that little bike, trying hard to keep up, trying my best not to let go.

We traversed the parking lot three times. Back and forth, back and forth, each trip ending with the same question, "You didn't let go, did you daddy?"

"Of course not!"

But she was ready. I knew it. She didn't.

And then it happened …

Ten feet into the fourth trip across the parking lot, when I knew she could do it, I let go. She had no idea she was pedaling on her own. I watched her ride as best I could through tear-filled eyes. She made it across to the other side. She didn't fall.

When she came to a stop she turned around and saw me standing on the other side of the parking lot.

"You let go!" she yelled.

"I couldn't keep up. You were riding too fast! Ride it back to me."

"I can't!"

"Yes, you can! You just rode it all across on your own."

And so she had. And so she would.

She was all smiles as she rode toward me. When she got to within a few feet she stopped, jumped off her bike and into my arms.

"I did it!"

"You did it! Let's go get mom and show her!"

She rode around in the parking lot in big circles for mom. We took photos to remember the moment. We celebrated with ice cream.

I didn't really let go. I set her free. I watched her grow.

May I Take Your Order?

One by one, the boys and girls in Miss Balistreri's second grade class walked to the front of the classroom, reached their tiny hands into a basket held high by their teacher, and pulled out a piece of paper. As they glanced down to reveal their choices, some of the boys high-fived each other and some of the girls giggled.

They had picked "teacher", "doctor", "nurse", "lawyer", "accountant", "journalist" and "auto mechanic". They picked "fire fighter", "police officer" and "court reporter". They picked "office manager", "welder" and "carpenter". One little girl picked "musician" and one little boy picked "veterinarian".

Our seven-year-old daughter glanced down at her paper and smiled. She neatly folded her paper and tucked it into the pocket in her skirt. She had picked "waitress".

They didn't know it, but they were participating in a long tradition of Nardin Academy second graders. It was a rite of passage. It was a peek into their futures. It was a chance to show them that their futures were unlimited and bright, that it was a big, beautiful world awaiting them and they could all be whatever they wanted to be.

They would have one whole week to prepare their presentations. They could ask questions of their parents and siblings and teacher. They could visit the library. They could visit places where their "choices" worked, like hospitals, restaurants, colleges, and stores. But the report they wrote had to be all their own.

This was a very big deal. This was the one day, near the end of the school year, when parents would be allowed into the classroom to watch the presentations. And we could bring camcorders! And the students could dress in costumes to match their chosen professions.

For the next six days our daughter peppered us with questions at home. We took her to a couple of restaurants too so she could see exactly what waitresses did. She acted out her part at family dinners, wearing a uniform, handing out menus she had made to her mom, dad, papa, and mama. She even gave a menu to her puppy. Her papa always ordered a hamburger because that was always on the "Daily Specials" menu.

I always ordered Bananas Foster for dessert, and she always frowned and told me, "I'm sorry sir, but we just ran out of Bananas Foster. You can have ice cream instead".

She would carefully write down every customer order and run them into the kitchen and hand them to her mom. She would run back and forth, filling our water glasses, delivering our orders, and asking us how everything was tasting. She even gave us the dinner check and told us to take our time in paying! I always gave her a two-dollar tip.

Such is the great joy of being a kid and even greater joy of being a parent.

Our young girl was no stranger to food and cuisine. She watched Chef Emeril Lagasse on TV with me, and she wouldn't go to bed until she watched every episode of Two Hot Tamales with celebrity chefs Mary Sue Milliken and Susan Feniger. She had her own apron and chef's hat and helped me prepare mushroom duxelles for Beef Wellington. She helped me prepare potato-crusted red snapper too. She helped her mom mash potatoes and she helped me fill buns with hot dogs off the grill. She loved to study cookbooks and menus at restaurants, and she paid attention.

She worked all weekend on her report. It was six pages long, 188 words, and she would have to read those words aloud to her teacher and classmates. Her capital letters were one inch high, and her lower-case letters half that. She spent hours making it perfect.

We drove our young waitress to school on Tuesday morning as she guarded her report in her navy-blue Kipling backpack – the one adorned with little monkeys. She didn't really need the report. She didn't know it, but she had memorized it. She practiced her presentation all the way to school that day.

It was a packed classroom – twenty kids took their seats and even more beaming parents stood in a semi-circle around the perimeter. Miss Balistreri got started right away, welcoming the parents and calling the students up to the front of the classroom. One by one, each student sat next to their teacher facing their classmates and parents. She introduced each student by name and announced the profession and career we were about to learn about. One by one, we were enlightened and entertained by those bright young kids. One by one, a parent would take a few steps forward to get a better view and press "Record" on a camcorder.

One student, dressed in blue hospital scrubs with a stethoscope around his neck, told us what it was like to be a doctor. One student wore a tool belt around her waist and carried a hammer. She explained how a carpenter built houses. Another brought a guitar. It was a mix of Halloween and Broadway. The youngsters were excited, and some were anxious. The parents were all beaming with pride. All were smiling, some shed tears, me among them.

And then it happened …

"Waitress"
by Adelina Simpson, Age 7

"A waitress serves food and drink in a restaurant.

Some of a waitress's duties are taking reservations, preparing tables, taking customers to their tables, handing out menus, answering questions, describing specials not on the menu, taking orders, serving food and drinks, and clearing the tables.

A waitress may also prepare the bill and collect the money.

A waitress must also be friendly, helpful, and polite, able to work well and remain calm under pressure.

There is no special schooling needed for the job of a waitress.

Waitresses learn their skills on the job.

Waitresses work under the direction of a manager or maitre'd.

A waitress would read specials like this to the customers:

Tonight, the Chef has prepared:

First Course
Jumbo Lump Crab and Gulf Shrimp

Second Course
Sea Scallop with Smoked Salmon Pasta, Basil Cream and Caper Relish

Third Course
House Smoked Duck in Baby Pumpkin with Cranberry Glace

Fourth Course
Grilled Steak with Parmesan Mashed Potatoes, Broccoli, and Cherry Tomatoes

Fifth Course
Cheese with Red Flame Grapes

Sixth Course
Sweet Rice Pudding with Dried Cherries and Apricots in a Pastry Crust

May I take your order?"

As she spoke her last few words, a collective, audible "Aww" filled the classroom. She wowed them with a copy of a tasting menu from our visit to Emeril Lagasse's restaurant in New Orleans. There were a lot of "Awws" that day.

The years go by quickly, too quickly for parents. Our daughter never worked as a waitress. But I am sure she always treats them well. I am sure she always leaves them a nice tip. She knows how hard they work. I wonder if she knows that, whenever her mom and I sit across from her at a restaurant and watch her order, we sometimes drift off to that morning of long ago in her second-grade classroom on Cleveland Avenue. And then we smile. We were so proud of her then and even prouder now.

Thank you, Miss Balistreri! You gave us a memory to last a lifetime.

May I take your order?

We'll See ...

A few days ago, my daughter sent me a photo of a very cool old-time AM/FM radio in a real walnut wood enclosure. I'm not sure why she sent it. Maybe it was because she knows how much I love gadgets, and especially radios. But maybe, I thought, it was because she's got my genes. Maybe she loves this stuff as much as I do!

So, I did what any dad would do for his daughter. I found it online and ordered it for her for Father's Day! She told me I got it backwards – that she was supposed to give me a gift for Father's Day. Someday, when she is a mom, she'll understand that making his daughter happy is the greatest gift a dad can receive.

I just had to buy her this radio. I didn't even give her a chance to ask me for it.

The need to buy that radio probably comes from my childhood.

Whenever I showed my dad something I wanted in the Century or Brand Names catalog – something that I really, really, really needed and couldn't live without, he would just study the picture for ten whole seconds and then look me square in the eye and say, "We'll see!"

He said, "We'll see," a lot.

I knew he was going to give my request a lot of deep, serious thought when he said, "We'll see."

And I gave him a lot to think about. I made a list, updated it often, and kept it under my pillow for years. There was an official Spalding signed Johnny Unitas genuine leather football, a Lionel train, and an AIWA 3-inch reel-to-reel tape recorder on that list. There was a yellow Schwinn SuperSport 10-speed bike, an Eldon 1/32 scale racing car set, and an in-ground swimming pool on that list too. And there were two puppies, three kittens, a full-grown Great Dane and a goldfish on the list of things that I absolutely needed when I was ten years old.

My dad was always thinking hard about the things on my list. But he had a lot of other things on his mind too. He was always working hard to put "food on our table" and a "roof over our heads" so I didn't bother him too much about my list. I knew he was doing this stuff because he told me in those exact words.

When I would ask him when I might get my Joe Pepitone official New York Yankees first baseman's mitt, or my 32-inch Mickey Mantle Louisville Slugger, he would always tell me that I would get it on "the second Tuesday of next week!" That was good enough for me. I spent a lot of time shopping for calendars with lots of Tuesdays in them.

I would get very excited when he would head out the front door and get in his car on a Saturday morning. I would chase after him. I was sure he was heading to the store to surprise me. He would roll down the window and I would ask, "Where are you going dad?"

"Timbuktu! Want to come?"

My dad went to Timbuktu a lot. He went there almost every weekend. But Timbuktu was scary to a kid. I had seen a lot of Tarzan movies and I was pretty sure there were lions and tigers in Timbuktu, so I respectfully declined.

Most of the things on my list stayed there for years – like the Louisville Slugger baseball bat. I asked for it when I was ten, and again when I was eleven. At age twelve I played most of the season at first base for the Tavano Insurance Pirates using a bat that I borrowed from a teammate.

And then it happened ...

I made the North End Little League All-Star Team! Coach Shimmel told me I was going to be the starting first baseman.

At dinner that night my mom served up some angel food cake with strawberries and whipped cream for dessert – and it wasn't even my birthday! And then my dad brought out a surprise present wrapped in paper covered with baseballs. It was the Louisville Slugger baseball bat signed by Mickey Mantle that I had been dreaming about for years! It cost $5.79, money that I knew my dad didn't have. He was washing the dinner dishes when my mom took me aside in the living room. "Your father has been saving his money for the whole little league season to buy that bat for you." I knew then that I would hit every ball the pitcher threw at me.

It wasn't the last time my dad would come through. When I was fifteen years old I rode to Ellicottville from Niagara Falls on my broken-down, second-hand three-speed bicycle with Steve Miller and Mark Aiduk. My derailleur cable broke in Springville, and I had to wedge a stone in the derailleur and tie it up with string and tape to hold it together. I rode twenty miles up and down the hills on the old Route 219 in first gear! I was so tired when we got to my Uncle Ernie's cabin that I was sure he would have to adopt me and let me move in with him for keeps.

But, early the next morning, just as we were finishing breakfast, we heard a car beeping its horn coming down Cotter Road and stirring up a world of dust. It was a blue Ford Galaxy 500. It was my dad. He opened the back door of the car and there it was, a shiny new three-speed bicycle from Sears & Roebuck!

I didn't ask my dad for that bike. But he knew I really, really needed it.

My daughter didn't ask me for that radio. I'm not sure she really, really needed it.

We'll see ...

How Do You Know?

Bob: "Sweetheart, I've been wondering, 'How do you know?'"

Ellen: "Know what?"

Bob: "When you meet for the first time, but it feels like you've known each other forever ..."

Ellen: "Whatever ..."

Bob: "When conversations last for minutes, then hours, then days, then a lifetime ..."

Ellen: "This sounds like a soliloquy – can you please go deliver your speech in another room?"

Bob: "When she asks you a question, but you need not respond, because she sees your answer in your eyes ..."

Ellen: "I'm smarter than you and you know it. I already knew both the question and the answer ..."

Bob: "When forgiveness comes quickly, and arguments don't last ..."

Ellen: "You do a lot of dumb stuff. Life is short. I have to forgive you quickly ..."

Bob: "When she laughs at your jokes when no one else does ..."

Ellen: "Someone has to ... I've seen you cry ...

Bob: "When she listens to your stories and doesn't let on that she has heard them all before ..."

Ellen: "I'm not really listening. I'm watching Forensic Files and learning about arsenic ..."

Bob: "When she nurses you when you are sick and laughs with you when you are well ..."

Ellen: "You've taken that 'in sickness and in health' thing a bit too far to the Catholic side ..."

Bob: "When she greets you in the morning with a smile and says goodnight with a kiss …"

Ellen: "You may be confusing me with our dogs …"

Bob: "When she gives you a hug and it feels like she will never let go …"

Ellen: "You were on your way to Best Buy – I had no choice …"

Bob: "When it's raining outside, but there's sunshine in your heart …"

Ellen: "You are not going to mention your snoring are you …"

Bob: "When two minds share a single thought, and two hearts beat as one …"

Ellen: "If your single thought is what I think it is you should go take a cold shower …"

Bob: "When your see her beauty in your daughter's eyes, the greatest gift of all …"

Ellen: "OK, OK, you just won me over, you can stop talking now ..."

Bob: "When the whole world is crashing around you, but you still have each other …"

Ellen: "And the dogs, don't forget our dogs!"

Bob: "When you can't carry a tune, but you sing that love song from the highest mountain …"

Ellen: "Please don't sing!"

Bob: "But I love you!"

Ellen: "Ditto ..."

Bob: "Ditto??? That's all you've got???"

Ellen: "Ditto ..."

Bob: "I love you Ellen..."

Ellen: "I love you Bob..."

Bob: "Ditto ... That's how you know that it's true love."

How I Love You

Like the morning loves the sun;
Like the evening loves the moon;
That's how I love you.

Like the autumn loves the leaves;
Like the winter loves the snow;
That's how I love you.

Like the flower loves the rain;
Like the willow loves the wind;
That's how I love you.

Like a puppy loves a boy;
Like a kitten loves a girl;
That's how I love you.

Like a secret loves a whisper;
Like a joke loves a laugh;
That's how I love you.

Like a reader loves a book;
Like a writer loves a word;
   That's how I love you.

Like a poet loves a poem;
Like a singer loves a song;
   That's how I love you.

Like a husband loves his wife;
   That's how I love you!

631-0865

It was an early spring evening, April 17, 1982, in Western New York. Two hundred and fifty guests joined the wedding party for the reception at Samuel's Grande Manor. I attended the reception alone, not because I couldn't find a date, but because the bride asked me not to. Sally had other plans for me that evening and, as it turns out, for the rest of my life.

I've told most of this story before, but not this part. It has taken me nearly six and a half decades of living to admit it, although I've hinted at it from time to time. I have a fear of telephones. I have a fear of using them, especially if the number I am calling is connected to a beautiful woman on the other end.

I didn't fear talking to her at the reception. We spoke for hours, as if we had known one another forever. Love is like that I guess – words flow like a stream after a storm when Cupid strikes. I didn't fear asking her to dance either. It wasn't hard to ask the most beautiful woman in the room to dance to "Beautiful" by Gordon Lightfoot. But, at the end of the most magical evening of my life 'til then, as the wedding guests were leaving the dance floor and heading to their cars, as our words were drifting towards "good-by", and as my inner voice was begging me to "ask her", I faltered. I am not sure why I didn't ask her for her phone number. I am sure that men more confident than me would have. Perhaps I feared rejection. Or perhaps I enjoyed a challenge.

It took exactly thirty six hours to muster the courage. On Monday morning I found her father's office phone number in the phone book. I was at my desk at my job. I waited and worried. I braced myself for rejection. I dialed six of the seven digits and hung up the phone. I did this a few times before letting it ring.

"Doctors' office," the receptionist answered, "how may I help you?"

"Hi, I'm Bob and this is a different kind of a call to your office," I said. "You see, I was at a wedding this past Saturday, and the doctor was there, and I met his daughter, and we talked for a few hours, and her brother interrogated me, and we danced together to "Beautiful" by Gordon Lightfoot, not her brother and me, but she and me, and I would love to call her and ask her for a date, but I forgot to ask her for her phone number, and her brother asked me what kind of car I drive and what my job is and what my annual income is, and what my religion is, and whether I am a Republican or Democrat ..."

I rambled on and on for about ten minutes. I didn't want to stop talking for fear of rejection. But, the courage surfaced, "So I was wondering if you could somehow call her and tell her that this guy, Bob, called, and maybe tell her that I really enjoyed meeting her, and was wondering if she would possibly consider giving you her phone number to give to me so I could call her?"

"Sure honey, I'll check this out for you. Just give me your phone number and I'll get back to you."

I am sure the receptionist, Ann, was smiling and even giggling through that entire phone call. I am sure, because she later told me, that she talked about that call with her co-workers the rest of that day. And, I am sure that she relayed my message, as best as she could remember it, to the most beautiful woman at that Saturday wedding reception.

I skipped lunch that day at the office. I just sat at my desk, sweating, looking at my telephone, wishing it would ring. Minutes turned to hours, anticipation turned to hope, and hope started to fade. Perhaps she wasn't interested. Perhaps she would have been interested if I had had the courage to ask her for her phone number myself, in person, that evening.

And then it happened …

The phone rang at 2:56 p.m.

"Hi honey, this is Ann from the doctor's office. I talked to Ellen about her phone number."

And then she paused. It was an excruciating pause of maybe two whole seconds.

"Honey, do you have a piece of paper and pencil handy?"

"Yes, I do."

"Ok, great, her office number is 634-0044; her home number is 631-9951, and she asked me to let you know that her private number for the phone in her bedroom is **631-0865**."

"Thank you, Ann!"

"Good luck, honey!"

It's funny how a phone call like that can change your whole outlook on life. It can turn fear into confidence in an instant. It can ease your mind and bring on a smile. I've never scored a touchdown in a Super Bowl but I imagine it feels a lot like it does when a beautiful woman gives you her private phone number.

And then I called ...

And then we became friends ...

And then we dated ...

And then we married ...

Ellen transferred that private phone number to our house right after we got married. We kept it for a few months and then gave it up to save money. We never thought much about it after that. We went to law school, started new careers, brought a beautiful daughter into the world, and lived life. One day, with my brother and hers, we started a software company out of our home. We automated all the forms that patent and trademark lawyers use. It was a great small business.

But, a week before we opened our home business, more than ten years after we disconnected Ellen's private phone number, she called the phone company to ask for a new phone number for our new business.

And then it happened …

"Do you have a piece of paper and pencil handy?
"Yes, I do."
"Then write this down. Your new office phone number is **631-0865**!" Ellen gasped. It was her old private phone number that she had given up a decade ago!

What are the odds!? I have no idea. But we have been smiling ever since.

Ellen later told me that she wasn't concerned that I hadn't asked for her phone number at the reception. She told me that somehow she knew that I would find her and that we would meet again. Some things, like phone numbers and true love, are meant to be.

I Never Knew

It was a simpler time. It was a time of innocence. It was a time I dearly miss.

I met him at a school playground. I was seven years old. Lewis was seven and a half. He had an ever-present infectious smile. He was always happy. We became fast friends. I don't know why or how. We just did. We did everything together. We were inseparable.

We didn't live close to one another. I had to walk ten city blocks to get to his house on Saturdays and he did the same to get to mine on Sundays. During the hot summer days in Niagara Falls we would meet in the middle at Gluck Park. We played baseball and basketball together. We rode our bikes around the city together. Sometimes we would stand next to each other behind a crack in a sidewalk and pretend we were Olympic sprinters. A friend would yell, "Runners, take your mark, get set, go!" and off we would race, imagining we were in a stadium full of cheering spectators. Sometimes I would win; sometimes Lewis would win; always we both would win, although we didn't know it.

In the fall we would play football together. Lewis would be the quarterback and I would be the wide receiver. We would score imaginary touchdowns in NFL stadiums on every play. We would never lose. We couldn't lose. We were best friends.

We wrestled together in the soft grass atop the fallen leaves. He always pinned me. He always made me say "Uncle". And then he would let me up with a laugh. He always won. I always lost. But really we both won, although we didn't realize it then.

When the weather turned cold, and the snow began to fall we would don our boots and gloves and trek through the snowbanks to meet and play. Wind and snow couldn't keep us apart. We would still race each other on those frigid days – on ice skates on backyard rinks.

I remember the first time Lewis invited me inside his

home on one of those cold winter days. He introduced me to his mom. She called me "Robert" and smiled. She served us hot chicken soup and sandwiches.

I remember the first time I invited Lewis inside my home. I introduced him to my mom. She called him "Lewis" just like me, even though most of his friends called him "Bubby". She smiled at us as she served us tomato soup, grilled cheese sandwiches and homemade chocolate pudding with whipped cream. Then we learned how to play chess together on a red and black cardboard chessboard with black and white plastic pieces. We played chess for hours on those cold winter days. Sometimes I would win; sometimes Lewis would win; always we both would win, although we didn't know it.

And then it happened ...

Elementary school ended and so did a part of our childhoods. We went to different junior high schools and different high schools. We drifted apart. We never played chess together again. We never tossed the football again or raced each other down the city streets. I never saw his smile again. I thought about him now and again and I hoped he thought about me and our friendship too. I tried to find him every now and then but never did. I heard he went undefeated as a wrestler in high school. I'll bet he let his opponents up with a laugh when they cried "Uncle"!

I heard he joined the Navy. I imagined that he never stopped smiling. I heard he went to heaven about ten years ago.

I never knew.

I never knew Lewis was Black.

And I'm pretty sure he never knew I was White.

We just knew we were friends – best friends.

(In memory of Lewis Jerome "Bubby" Sconiers, 1955-2010, Niagara Falls, New York)

You Can Still Love

She was tall and slender and pretty. When I was a young boy of three and would tug on the pockets of her apron to ask for a cookie, she was twice as tall as the kitchen stove. When you can't see the top of the stove yourself your mom seems as tall as a giraffe.

That image of her in our kitchen looking down at me while standing over the stove will never leave me. It is frozen in living color in my mind's eye.

Mom and Robert (holding a cookie)
at kitchen table - circa 1959

I can still smell the aroma of her French-Canadian butter tarts – I can still almost taste them in my dreams.

And I still remember her asking me to help her with the scraps of dough left over from her lemon meringue pie crust.

"What are we making mom?" I would ask as we sprinkled cinnamon sugar on the dough, sliced them into strips, and rolled them up before baking them.

"They are 'pets de Souers,'" she replied.

"What does that mean mom?"

"I will tell you when you are older," she promised.

Even then she had a "bad arm". She didn't talk about it much. She would just grimace if you tugged on it a little too hard. She never told me how much it really hurt or that sometimes it would just tingle. She never told me that sometimes she couldn't feel her arm at all. And she never, ever told me that the family doctor had given her pills to ease the pain so that she could sleep. She never told me how much it hurt to play catch with a baseball with her oldest son in the backyard on a hot summer day.

You can still play a game of catch with your child even if you are sick.

She would come to all of my little league baseball and tyro football games when I was a young athlete. She never missed a game. She would always tell me how great she thought I played even if my team lost. Sometimes she would leave the games early. I never knew why.

You can still watch your child's ball games even if you are sick.

She would quiz me on my Spanish vocabulary words in junior high school. She would sit in her chair with me on the couch, for as long as it took, day after day, week after week. She wouldn't stop until I memorized them all, backwards and forwards. Sometimes she would groan and then run to the medicine chest with a glass of water. I never knew why.

You can still help your child with his homework even if you are sick.

She walked thirteen city blocks to watch me give a speech on stage in the eighth grade when I ran for student council president. She didn't tell me she was coming. She didn't tell me how much it hurt to walk that far. She never told me that my dad made dinner for us that night because she was in such pain.

You can still walk a mile to hear your child give a speech even if you are sick.

And then it happened ...

I remember the day in tenth grade like it was yesterday. I was sixteen years old. My mom was forty-nine. They broke the news to us as gently as they could. "Mom needs surgery," our dad told us. "They have to fix her neck."

"What's wrong?" we asked.

"It's 'syringomyelia,'" my mom replied.

She never told us how rare the disease was or that it would slowly paralyze her, starting at her extremities and working its way to her core. Surely, she knew. She was the smartest person I ever knew. But all she ever told me was that dad would be doing all the cooking and cleaning in our house from then on.

You can still comfort and protect your child even when you are sick.

From that day forward my dad worked all day and then came home and prepared all the family dinners. He did the laundry and cleaned the house too. All the while, he took care of the love of his life as best he could. We would all pitch in and cut the grass and shovel the snow and eventually we learned how to do our own laundry and do a little cooking too. But not as well as mom.

"It needs more salt!" she would yell from her chair, or later from her bed, as her condition worsened.

You can still teach your husband how to cook, and your kids too, even when you are sick.

By the time I graduated from high school she wore a constant brace around her neck to support her head. She was in constant pain but never told me. She stood tall next to my dad and me, in my cap and gown, on the front lawn for photos on my graduation day.

You can still show your child how proud you are even if you are sick.

By the time I graduated from college she was in a wheelchair most of the time. My dad had built a cart in our garage to transport her from her bed to her chair in the morning, and back to bed in the evening. She still played Jeopardy along with the TV contestants every night. And she usually won.

You can still keep learning and teaching your grown kids lessons even if you are sick.

By the time I got married she could no longer walk and could stand for only a few minutes. But she could steal your heart with a beaming smile as she entered the church down the center aisle on your wedding day, pushed in a wheelchair by your best man – her youngest son. And nothing in this world, no illness, no disease, no paralysis, could stop her from standing for a few seconds for the mother-son dance at your wedding reception.

You can still dance with your son at his wedding, even if you can't move your feet, even if you are sick.

By the time I graduated from law school she was spending half of her time in bed and half of her time in a living room chair. My brother and I built a wheelchair ramp for her so she could visit our relatives. She used it a lot from September to December – buying Christmas presents for her children and grandchildren. On Christmas Day the whole family would gather as she would pass out present after present and laugh and sing.

You can still spread the spirit of Christmas even if

you are sick.

And then it happened …

I was enjoying my birthday cake when I received the call. I had seen her just a week before. I had spoken to her by phone just the day before. She told me she loved me. I told her I loved her too.

I kissed her good-bye for the last time on the evening of my forty-seventh birthday. I still blow kisses to her even now.

She still makes me laugh. I looked it up just the other day, "pets de Souers" is French for "farts of nuns". I'm glad you never told me mom.

You can still love, and you can still laugh, even when you are sick.

*Niagara Falls
High School
Eighty Sixth Annual
Commencement
Class of 1974*

*Niagara Falls
International
Convention Center*

*Sunday, June
Twenty-Third
One O'Clock*

The Gold Button

At Hyde Park Elementary School in the 1960s, you had to pass eight physical fitness tests to earn the Blue Button, fifteen tests to earn the Silver Button, and twenty tests to earn the Gold Button. Our gym teachers, Mr. Gietz and Miss Miller showed us the shiny buttons on the first day of gym class in fourth grade. We even got to hold them in our hands before we passed them to our classmates. I didn't want to let go of the Gold Button. I remember kissing it and whispering, "Someday you will be mine!"

These buttons were a really big deal – it was the Olympics of elementary school. Underclassmen like second and third graders weren't allowed to take the tests for the buttons, probably because the teachers were afraid the kids would fall off the ropes suspended from the ceiling or bounce off the trampoline into outer space. Plus, little kids always seemed to cry a lot when they fell down, especially off the balance beam. They would even cry if they just lost a race. It was good school policy to make them wait to try to earn a button until they were as mature as my friends and me in the fourth grade.

Mr. Gietz and Miss Miller explained to us in our first gym class that physical fitness was very important – that it was as important as schoolwork. They told us that the late President Kennedy had designed the tests himself and ordered all the schools to give out these buttons, so I knew it was important. I loved President Kennedy, and all my friends did too. I imagined that he probably wore his Gold Button around the White House. If the president wanted me to be physically fit, I was all in. Plus, they explained to us that it wasn't about winning and losing, it was about trying, and they always encouraged us to try our best, and never made us feel bad if we failed. They taught us, "to win without boasting, and lose without excuse."

These tests were designed to test every aspect of a kid's physical fitness. And I believed that every test had a purpose and a possible function in real life. Take the 50-yard dash, for example. One time I planted a hidden microphone in the basement of our house, and I overheard my older sister, Mary, tell her boyfriend, Frank, that she loved him. I turned on my hidden speaker and announced, "I love you too Mary – maybe we should get married!" My sister was pretty fast, for a girl. She got to the top of the basement stairs and grabbed a cast iron skillet from the cupboard just as I was leaving the house through the front door. As she chased me down Niagara Avenue, skillet in hand raised over her head, I remember feeling very happy that I could run a 50-yard dash in 6.5

seconds ... and she couldn't!

It was hard to pass all the tests during the school year. Since there were twenty tests total, and we had gym class twice a week, you only got a few chances to try and pass each test during the year. And some of the tests were "outside" tests – like the softball throw and the 600-yard run – you couldn't do those during the winter.

Talk about a useful physical fitness test – the softball throw has to be at the top of the list. Just ask my boyhood friend, Timmy Bax, who made the mistake of forgetting to call "dibs on windows" just before he threw a softball through a window of Mrs. Brown's kindergarten classroom. I liked Timmy. We all did. But we scattered like sheep without a shepherd after Tim's errant pitch in fourth grade. My poor friend was still paying for that window out of his allowance in sixth grade and visiting his probation officer every other Sunday in the summer. Oh, and about that word "dibs" - don't bother looking it up. In the North End, "dibs" came from the Latin for, "if you break a window with a flying projectile that left your hand, not only are we not helping you to pay for it, but we are all pointing at you when our parents ask who did it!" In our neighborhood sandlot games, just before alternating our hands on the handle of a baseball bat to see who got to pick players for their team first, we all yelled "no dibs on windows" in unison.

But I digress – back to the tests and my unusual

pre-puberty athletic prowess. I was the first kid in the fourth grade to win the Blue button. I passed every test Mr. Gietz threw my way that year: 50-yard dash, vertical jump, standing broad jump, flip on a trampoline …. My eighth test was chin-ups. Today they call these "pull-ups" but in my school we called them chin-ups on account of my friend Joey Forgione who did six in a row and then decided to rest a while with his chin on the bar. Joey was stuck there for about an hour before we realized he couldn't talk and ask for help, but he recovered before he started the fifth grade.

Mr. Gietz sure made you feel special when you won a button. He blew his whistle really loudly and that silenced everyone. Then he said, "Kids, gather round." We all sat on the floor around him and Miss Miller in anticipation. Then he would reach into his bag for the button and call your name. You couldn't help but walk up to him smiling ear to ear as he pinned the button on your shirt. Miss Miller bestowed the same honor on the girls. I was beaming when Mr. Gietz gave me my Blue button in front of all my friends, and I ran all the way home from school that day to show my mom.

I slept with my Blue button on my pillow the whole summer between fourth and fifth grade. I think a bunch of my friends slept with theirs too. I knew it wasn't that big a deal – it was only eight tests, and the button was inexplicably Blue. I always thought it should have been

Bronze. I didn't wear it publicly, of course, because I didn't want to show off, but I wore it around my house. Once I had the Blue, I set my sights on Silver, and practiced running and jumping all that summer.

You could only practice some of the tests easily on your own. One test that was especially problematic was the vertical rope climb. I thought long and hard about the rationale behind this test. As every kid in gym class knows, when they built the school, the construction guys left some really thick, and really long ropes hanging from the ceiling in the gym. No one knows why they were there or why there was a big knot at the bottom of each one. We kids thought they probably played Tarzan with them. There were four ropes in a row, so we were pretty sure they pretended they were in a jungle and swung from one rope to the next. This was by far the hardest test for most kids, and sometimes the most embarrassing. The idea was to climb all the way up the rope to the top, and then climb all the way back down without getting brush-burns on your hands. And we did this while being serenaded to "go you chicken fat go" on the loudspeaker. I remember feeling sorry for some of the chubby kids who would just stand on the knot with a sad face. But somehow Mr. Gietz always made those kids laugh and not feel bad. He used to gently push them like they were on a swing until they started to giggle. I also felt bad for the kids with acrophobia. It was a big mistake to look down when you got to the top, and I never understood why we didn't have nets, or at least firemen waiting to catch us at the bottom.

I asked Mr. Gietz what use this test would have in my future life as a lawyer, but he didn't seem to want to answer me. He mumbled something about the Army and basic training, but I really didn't understand him, so I didn't ask again. I just figured he needed time to think about it some more.

It took a whole month in the summer for my next-door neighbor, Gary McLaughlin, and me to figure out how to train outside of school for this test. It turns out that, if your bedroom is on the second floor of your house, you can tie one end of a rope around your bed post, throw the other end out an open window, and then practice climbing down the rope in the middle of the night after your parents have gone to bed. This was

Gary's idea (that's what I told my mom.) Once you climb down, it is best to rest a little before climbing back up. You have to find stuff to do before your ascent. We used to eat green tomatoes and rhubarb out of Mrs. Miller's garden (no relation to our gym teacher) to pass the time before our ascent, and then practice running the 50-yard dash when the Millers' dog started to bark. I don't know why rhubarb and green tomatoes taste so good when you pluck them out of someone else's garden in the middle of the night. But I do know it's important to climb back into your room real soon after dining, because too much rhubarb and too many green tomatoes can give you a stomachache.

By the time fifth grade began, I was totally in shape and ready for gym class. I passed test after test as the months ticked by. I climbed the rope to the ceiling in 3.6 seconds to thunderous applause and came down just as fast. I kept a chart on my bedroom wall and marked off my achievements. My dad told me not to brag, but now that I've had my right knee replaced, I hope you don't mind if I mention that I earned my Silver button in May of my penultimate year of elementary school. That's right – I was the first fifth-grader to earn Silver, and my night-time dreams were of Gold in the Olympics.

Sixth grade started with a bang, and, as long as I'm bragging, I don't mind telling you about my best event in sixth grade – the 600-yard run. The starting point was behind the fence around the playground in the back of the school, at 27th and Linwood. There were thirty kids all bunched up at the starting line jockeying for position. There was a blue line painted on the sidewalk. You were sunk if you were in the back. That's where Jim Perez was. We ran for the first time in September right after Labor Day. Mr. Gietz blew his whistle and I bolted out in front and never looked back. I imagined all the people in cars on Hyde Park Boulevard were watching me as I ran the length of the school in the front of the building. I felt like Jesse Owens. You had to pace yourself in this race. It was one and a half times around the school. By the time I was back at the finish line I was fifty yards ahead of my closest classmate. On the home stretch I actually lapped some of my friends, and I heard Jim yell, "go you chicken fat go." I finished in one minute and fifty-one seconds, a record for the sixth grade that year. And my friend, Rosemary Paolone, finished in two minutes and two seconds, a record for the girls.

In the Spring, Mr. Gietz announced on the school PA system that Rosemary and I would be running the 600 again, but this time just the two of us, and we would be trying to set a school record. This time when we ran, the whole student body was looking out the classroom windows and rooting us on. I ran a 1:49, five seconds off the record, but Rosemary ran a 1:59, one of the few girls up to that time to break the two-minute barrier. And she was nice too.

It's funny how those tests played out, and how comforting and helpful a kid's parents and siblings can be. There is really no rhyme or reason as to what things a kid can do, and what things give him trouble. It is a genuine puzzle as to how an athletic sixth grader like me could run so fast and yet hit a plateau in October at nineteen tests passed, and not be able to master a simple test that everyone else seemed to pass with ease. For some reason, I just could not stand on my head, a disability that I was sure would haunt me in later life. And it wasn't for lack of practice. My younger brother, Michael, tried to help me. He threw a rope over a tree branch, tied one end around my ankles and then got five of his friends to pull hard until they hoisted me upside down a few inches above the ground. "OK, stand on your head, now!" he would yell just before he dropped me on my head. My parents were more helpful. They would hold me upside down on my bed until I seemed to have it. At least those falls were softer.

The big day was in early May. Mr. Gietz announced at the 10 a.m. gym class that this would be the last opportunity for the sixth graders to stand on their heads. The gym floor looked like the top of a birthday cake with candles that morning, as all my friends instantly shot up upside down. I firmly placed my hands and forearms on the mat as my spotter, Marty Shimmel, watched. Then I rolled a little forward until my head hit the mat as I held a three-point stance. Then I slowly lifted my legs and pointed my toes toward the sky. I could hear the murmuring excitement of my friends as I held my pose for five seconds. They all knew what was at stake. I dropped my legs knowing that I had done it as Marty called Mr. Gietz over.

And then it happened …

"I didn't see it," Mr. Gietz said. "Do it again." You've got to be kidding me. I swallowed hard. Then he blew his whistle. He called all my classmates around in a circle around my mat. He didn't say another word, but his eyes and smile were telling me that if I did it once I could do it again. And I did. Once my toes were pointed skyward the whole class counted "1-2-3-4-5" and then applauded. I was awarded my Gold Button at 10:45 a.m. that morning. My good friend, Mike Barone, got his that afternoon. I don't know about Mike, but I still have mine somewhere. I think about it whenever the Olympics come around. And sometimes, just for fun, I stand on my head and read a book.

What a Jump George!

A few days ago, as many of us were grieving and heartbroken to learn of the early passing of our dear friend, Kathy, I noticed the name of a person leaving her family a note of condolence on our high school Facebook page. I hadn't seen this name in more than fifty years!

So, I reached out to him with a private message.

"Are you 7' 11" George?"

I knew that if he was the George Stephens that I remembered, he would know exactly what I was talking about. And if he wasn't — he would write me off as a nutcase!

George responded. It was him!

I only met George once, on a hot summer day in 1967. I was eleven years old and so was George. I had been practicing the standing broad jump all summer long on the sidewalk in front of my house. I had already set the fifth grade record for the jump at Hyde Park Elementary School that year, but this was the big time - this was the AAU Junior Olympics!

It was a hot Tuesday, August 15, 1967, at Hyde Park

Stadium. There were 286 young athletes in the stadium from all over the city that day, competing for medals and ribbons. Every playground in the city was represented. The stands were filled with moms, dads, sisters, brothers and grandparents of the athletes. The firefighters who sponsored the Olympics awarded jackets to all the individual winners, and gave bicycles to 10 lucky boys and girls picked at random.

I remember being the first jumper to leap that day. And I soared - a personal best of 6'11", even beating my fifth grade record of 6'5". I was sure I would win the gold!

The third jumper was a tall, skinny, redheaded kid named Jim O'Toole. I think he was Irish. I remember thinking that he should have been disqualified for having legs as long as a giraffe's. He hardly even jumped at all! He just did a little hop. And he bumped me into second place with a jump of 7'5".

We sat and watched as another ten kids tried to knock us off the podium, but nobody came close. There was just one kid left, a skinny, short little kid from the 10th Street playground. We all thought he was too short to even be in this event. He was quiet and shy and unassuming, just standing waiting his turn. He didn't even warm up like the rest of us.

And then it happened ...

George Stephens let go a jump for the ages! He flew through the air and into the heavens as our jaws dropped. We didn't think he was ever coming down. Little George jumped 7'11" that day. He tied his own city record. Not only did he set a Midget Division Record - he even beat the Junior Division Record of 7'9"!

A standing broad jump of almost eight feet from a little kid who wasn't even five feet tall is just plain obscene. To put it into perspective, if Kareem Abdul-Jabbar was laying down in the grass, George could have jumped right over him, head to toe, with nine inches to spare!

At first, I wasn't happy for George. I would be going home with a third-place ribbon because of him after all. But then I saw him smile. And then I realized that I had just witnessed something very special. I joined all the other kids in congratulating George. We all shook his hand, and he made a special point of congratulating all of us on our jumps. He even took the time to congratulate Vanita LaVerde, who won a third-place ribbon for the girls.

I took an immediate liking to George. I've told this story a hundred times over the years. My father always taught me to, "Win without boasting and lose without excuse!" I think my dad knew I would bump into special people like George someday.

I was so in awe of George's jump that day that I didn't notice until just yesterday that my name was in the same newspaper, on the same day, on the same page as George's! It turns out that I anchored the winning 220 yard relay team that day! I took home a gold medal! I was probably one of the eight fastest kids in the stadium that day. But it's funny. I don't remember breaking the tape or receiving my gold medal. I only remember watching George fly through the air. I only remember him smiling and shaking my hand.

Yep, George soared into the heavens that summer July day at the Junior Olympics in 1967. I don't know how he came to know my friend, Kathy. But she is in heaven now and I can't help but think that she is smiling at bringing us together again.

Smile, laugh, love, JUMP & remember!

Stephens, 11, Sets New Jump Mark

Eleven-year-old George Stephens of 10th Street playground broke the 10-year-old standing broad jump record for the Midget Division during an AAU Junior Olympics regional meet at DeFranco Park Thursday.

Stephens leaped seven feet, 11 inches to easily shatter the old mark of seven feet. Stephens' jump is also better than the Junior Division record of 7-9 set by Randy Humphries Wednesday.

Mackenna Avenue playground won the close meet 89 to 79 for 10th Street. Ashland Avenue playground had 16 and DeFranco 12.

The program is co-sponsored by the Uniformed Firefighters 714 and the Dept. of Recreation. Finals are set for Aug. 15 in Hyde Park Stadium.

Jesse James and the Lunch Lady

Jesse James was the toughest, meanest kid in the school. He lived on the wrong side of town. He wore a black leather jacket. He spoke in short sentences. He scowled if you wished him good morning.

We were all afraid of him. We all avoided him. As best we could.

But a kid's got to eat.

At Gaskill Junior High, lunches cost thirty-two cents or thirty-three cents – depending. For thirty-two cents you got fish sticks with white milk, and for thirty-three cents you got chocolate milk. It was sort of like vanilla or chocolate ice cream. These flavors latch onto you early on, maybe even in the womb, and they don't tend to ever let you go.

I was a chocolate milk kind of kid. And I'm a chocolate ice cream kind of man. I was thankful that my parents could afford that extra penny. Some of my friends couldn't and it made me sad. It made me share.

Lunch time should be a fun time for junior high schoolers. Learning algebra, science, history, English and Spanish is hard work. Talking in class in front of your friends is scary. And getting up the nerve to ask a girl to a dance is downright frightening.

Lunch and gym were our only escapes, or so they should have been.

But every day, for three long years, we walked slowly and fearfully through the cafeteria line. We grabbed our tray and utensils and napkins. Mrs. Fabiano smiled at us as we filled our plates. She served us two pieces of pepperoni pizza on Thursdays. She watched us take extra broccoli on Wednesdays that would never find its way to our stomachs. She told us to remember to come back up for an ice cream sandwich.

It should have been such fun. But there he was, at the end of the line, standing right next to the cashier. Our parents never gave us thirty-two cents or thirty-three cents exactly. They always gave us a quarter and a dime. Lucky kids got an extra dime for ice cream. And there it was. We gave our thirty-five cents to the lunch lady, and she threw our change on our tray. She threw three pennies next to our white milk carton, or two cents next to our chocolate milk carton.

And then came the question. Jesse stood tall and tough right next to the cashier. Jesse paid attention. Jesse knew every student customer by name – last name. He asked every kid the same question every day. He asked me the same question every school day for three years. "Simpson – you got two cent!" (Jesse always had an issue with singular and plural versions of nouns.) He asked this probing question as he and I both stared at the two Lincoln pennies on my tray!

Most kids said yes, and then gave Jesse their change. Not me. My answer was always the same, "Yes, Jesse, I have two cents, and you can't have them!" I said this as I held my fork like a farmer's pitchfork over my pennies and pointed at his belly. Jesse never got my pennies, but it wasn't because of my fork. It was because I played on the football team. My teammates were bigger and tougher than Jesse, and Jesse knew it.

I felt bad for my friends who didn't play football. They never got to stop at Signore's for penny candy on the way home from school. Jesse deprived them of that. I did a calculation one day. Assuming that most of the 600 kids in the school drank chocolate milk, and most of them donated their change to Jesse, he cleared $2,160 a year for three years! That's $6,480 by the time he graduated to senior high! That's like $25,000 in today's money! Jesse was rich!

I didn't like Jesse. None of my friends did either. He shouldn't have done what he did.

And then it happened ...

It was a few days before Christmas during my ninth grade year. I was shopping at the mall with my parents for some last minute gifts for my sisters and brother. The Salvation Army Colonel was ringing his bell next to his kettle as we left the mall. That's when it happened.

A tall, tough-looking kid from the wrong side of town walked up and unfurled his hand over the kettle. Ten one-hundred-dollar bills floated down from his open hand. He didn't think I saw him, but I did. He didn't think I recognized him, but I did. I caught him by surprise. He worried that I would ruin his image. I just smiled at him and said, "Merry Christmas Jesse!" "Merry Christmas Bob!"

The first day after the Christmas break, I meandered through the lunch line. For the first and only time in my junior high school life I grabbed a carton of white milk. The lunch lady threw three pennies toward my tray, but I caught them in my hand in mid-air. "Simpson – got three cent?" "Sure Jesse, here you go!" He smiled. Me too.

Yeah - Jesse was bad, but he wasn't all bad.

I Voted for Penny

Junior high school is a big adjustment for kids. Before we get there, we think our elementary school is the only one in the city, and our friends and teachers are pretty much the only people in the world. When you are in sixth grade walking down Hyde Park Boulevard, and Junior High kids are walking the same route, you just can't help but wonder what it's like on the other side of Linwood Avenue. I imagine Columbus must have had the same feeling crossing the ocean. We little guys would take a hard right into the school we had called home since kindergarten, but the seventh, eighth and ninth graders would just keep walking. I often paused at the front door of our school, squinting back at the sidewalk in the morning sun to catch a glimpse of them. They were so brave to cross Linwood, I thought to myself.

When you are half as tall as a junior high schooler you tend to notice things closer to your eye level. I paid close attention to the junior high kids as they walked. It was easy to do because they paid no attention to me. One thing I noticed right away was that they carried books to school – and not just one or two. It was usually three or four books, and they were kept together with a band. I wanted to carry books to school too but my third-grade teacher told me we weren't allowed to because we might drop them in a puddle. The exception, of course, were library books. We were always allowed to take as many as three books out of the library at one time. I always took the max allowed and carried all three home so I would look smart. My favorite book was The Black Stallion by Walter Farley, but close behind were books about Babe Ruth and Thomas Edison – the Wizard of Menlo Park. I liked wizards. But the story that made me cry was the one about Lou Gehrig.

I also noticed that the books they carried didn't look like ours. They all had brown wrappers around them. I suspected they were waterproof to protect the books from puddles. I so wanted to be ready for junior high that I would sneak brown grocery bags into my bedroom and cut out book covers for my library books. I would practice carrying them around the house. I don't think my mom knew I did this. If she did, she never mentioned it. The brown book covers weren't the only thing I noticed from my level. I noticed that all the boys carried books but not all the girls did. The girls who didn't carry any books always seemed to be walking next to boys who were carrying more books than their friends. And that wasn't the only junior high mystery we sixth graders noticed. Some of the girls wore boys' football jackets in the fall and winter – either that or there were a lot of girls in junior high named Mike and Tom. Junior high school was going to take some figuring out.

After a summer of fun swimming and playing baseball, our turn came to cross Linwood Avenue and keep on going. It was a brave new world. On our first day of walking to school we were almost late for two reasons. First, we spent way too much time in Signore's Delicatessen on Hyde Park and Pierce. This was better than Disneyland – penny candy at eye level and within easy reach. The owner was a brilliant businessman, putting a store on the only road to school, and then hanging a big CANDY sign in the window. His name was Mario Signore, but we always called him Mr. Signore. He always wore a sweater vest and a thin tie. He watched us like a hawk from behind the counter. Sometimes he seemed a little gruff. I learned the word "loiter" from Mr. Signore. He put the word "no" in front of "loitering". If you spent too much time admiring the candy selection without putting your hand in your pocket, he would ask you in an Italian accent, "You gonna buy somethin' or just look all day long?" At first, I was afraid of him but then a couple of times I caught him giving candy to some kids who didn't have any money. I spent a lot of my lunch money on behalf of the Signore children college fund in seventh grade. My favorite was a Nielson's Jersey Milk chocolate bar from Canada.

But that was only part of the reason we were late. Just as we thought we were getting to the right school, we all stopped and stared. Right across the street from the school was the darndest thing – the Statue of Liberty! How could that be? Did we take a wrong turn? We had to look twice but there it was plain as day. How and why it got moved from Liberty Island in New York City to Hyde Park in Niagara Falls was the subject of many seventh grade conversations on that first day of school.

Seventh grade started off badly for me. First, I got caught hurling spit balls through a straw at the kids in the front row every time Miss Kramer turned her back on us to write on the chalk board. That's when I learned the new word "detention." (Miss Kramer's father was my dentist and he didn't use Novocain, so I took it out on her.) Then I got caught throwing six Super Balls at one time in Miss Chryzan's math class. If you don't know what that is, it's an extremely elastic ball made of Zectron which contains the synthetic polymer polybutadiene as well as hydrated silica, zinc oxide, stearic acid, and other ingredients. Miss Chryzan wasn't very impressed with my explanation of what a Super Ball was and why I should be allowed to test it when she caught me, and she told me so as she marched me down to Mr. Goldstein's office for a "conversation."

I had a bad feeling from the get-go about our meeting in the principal's office. They seemed too friendly with one another, and I found out why. Miss Chryzan was Mr. Goldstein's niece. If you ask me, there ought to be a Board of Education rule against a math teacher being a niece of a principal. The odds were stacked against me. But this did give me a chance to practice my public speaking skills. The conversation went like this.

Mr. Goldstein: "Robert, why were you throwing Super Balls in class?"

Me: "I was bored."

Mr. Goldstein: "Why were you bored?"

Me: "Because I already know all the math that she is trying to teach us."

Miss Chryzan: "I highly doubt that, Robert."

Me: (I could think of nothing to say, so we enjoyed awkward silence.)

Our silence was broken when Mr. Goldstein suggested that, if I was so smart, why don't I just take the final exam now, and, if I pass, just take that as my final grade and go to gym instead of math class for the rest of the year. He didn't seem very sincere as he said it, so I jumped on the opportunity. "It's a deal," I exclaimed, before he could take it back.

The next day during math class, Miss Chryzan took me to the faculty lounge, sat me down and gave me the final exam. I gave her back my finished test in an hour. I showed her – I scored a perfect 100! I spent the rest of the year in gym class during second period, and fourth period too. Mr. Goldstein kept his word. I respected him for that, and Miss Chryzan seemed relieved to be rid of me.

I'm not sure if it was that math achievement or my skills in dodgeball which I perfected taking gym class twice every day, but by eighth grade I was pretty popular. Of course, it may have been my mustache.

In the spring of eighth grade, I learned that I was one of eight students nominated by our teachers to run for Student Council office. I'm sure I got nominated twice by my gym teacher, which carried the day. This was heady stuff to be nominated. We each gave a speech before a "carefully selected screening committee." This committee was comprised of existing Student Council officers, plus some special guests from the United Nations.

I gave a speech to the committee on citizenship and leadership, on account of I had won a citizenship award in fourth grade and was captain of my little league team, and my mom advised me that I should talk about something that I knew about first-hand. The first screening committee was the precursor to the cooking show "Chopped" on the Food Network. The committee members told us we all did a great job, but only four of us made it to the next round. I felt bad for the kids who were chopped.

I remember being happy that two girls and two boys made it through the first round of screening. I didn't

STUDENT COUNCIL *SPECIAL* BULLETIN   May 8,1970

TO BE READ AND POSTED IN ROLL CALL:

As most of you probably already know, the
process of screening your Student Council Officers nominees started yesterday. The people
you nominated appeared before a carefully
selected committee composed of students and
teachers and eight of them were chosen to
proceed to the final screening committee next
week (which will determine the candidates).
The following is the list of remaining nominees
in alphabetical order:

> Roberta Basta
>
> Jim Fasciano
>
> Pamela (Penny) Ferro
>
> Lynne Kukulka
>
> Kevin McCumber
>
> Silvana Nardelli
>
> Toni-Jean Pasqualichio
>
> Robert Simpson

me

know all of them well, but James, Penny and Roberta seemed like swell kids. The first kid's birthday party I ever got invited to was for James' brother, Nelson. I thought it was really nice that they invited me. And everybody liked Penny and Roberta – both of them had starring roles in the school musical, and I feared this airtime would give them insurmountable publicity in the election.

The four candidates who emerged got our names read over the school's PA system, just after the Pledge of Allegiance. The Pledge was usually read by the Student Council President himself. He was the only kid in school allowed to touch the microphone. I always wished he would sing, but all he ever did was talk. It was a big deal to get your name read over the PA system. It was something you would announce at dinner when your mom asked, "What happened at school today?"

We were all thrilled to see our names in print on that mimeographed pink piece of paper. Some of us had enjoyed the privilege of making copies in the mimeograph room, where the aroma could make you dizzy, but to actually see our names in print was an entirely different matter.

We all wished the honor had ended with the press release, but such was not to be.

The second screening committee was worse than the first, because there were teachers on the committee. I remember Mr. Harmon, the Student Council advisor, taking notes on a pad as each kid spoke. You didn't know if a lot of notes was good or bad. Mrs. Colucci smiled at me when I gave my speech – but she was so nice she smiled at everybody. The purpose of this committee was to decide who was going to run for each office – President and Vice President. Those were the only two offices in play for the four of us. The top two vote getters ran for President, and the bottom two ran for Vice President. They didn't tell us how many votes we got.

I don't remember the speeches any of us gave that day, but I remember thinking Penny and Roberta were going to clobber James and me. They were both smart and pretty. How could we compete with that? I was especially impressed with Penny's speech which emphasized her plan for better food in the cafeteria and installation of a big clock on the front of the school so we would know when to come into school in the morning. My platform was centered on more ice cream and chocolate milk for lunch every day and adding pepperoni to the pizza on Thursdays. The committee kept us waiting on pins and needles for 20 minutes while they decided: I would run for President against Penny, and Roberta would run for Vice President against James. The student body voted for a whole ticket. We combined our names and my team Sim-ba (Robert SIMpson and Roberta BAsta) was running against Penny's team Fer-Ame (Penny FERro and JAMEs Fasciano). My God, we were clever.

Campaigns were organized and friends chose sides. I don't know what was happening at Penny's house, but my garage on Niagara Avenue was turned into Sim-ba campaign headquarters. My sister Mary made a huge stuffed lion mascot for us, and her friend Angela Cavese suggested our theme song, "The Lion Sleeps Tonight" by the Tokens. I'm not going to name names because I know that some of Penny's best friends today worked on my campaign back then, and I suspect some of my friends worked for her as well, but I will tell you that Mark Aiduk was my campaign manager and Sandy Fabiano and JoAnne Rossi worked in my garage printing 500 Sim-ba campaign buttons out of paper to hand out in school. My campaign workers, at Mark's suggestion, learned all the words to our theme song and hummed the tune at every opportunity to plant subliminal messages in the voters' minds. Imagine a bunch of eighth graders humming

"The Lion Sleeps Tonight" theme song. It was all very exciting as the campaign took on a life of its own. It was also very humbling to find out at such a tender age just how many good friends I had.

But there was just one problem, and it is a secret I have carried with me to this day ...

I had mixed emotions about winning. It wasn't that I didn't think I would do a good job. It was because, from the day of the second screening committee speeches, I had developed a Big League, Full-Blown, Junior High School Crush, on my opponent. She was trying to break the glass ceiling in heretofore male dominated junior high school Student Council elections, and I admired her for that. She was smart, she was pretty, and she was articulate. And she had a platform. Sure, I had a stuffed lion mascot and a theme song, but ice cream and pepperoni seemed to pale in comparison to nutritional meals and a clock for the front of the school.

I remember being so conflicted that I had trouble falling asleep at night during the campaign. In the mighty jungle the lion may have slept just fine, but I laid awake dreaming about Penny! It was fourth grade all over again. I was trying to beat the girl I was sure I was going to marry.

Election Day itself was the most exciting day in my life to that point. One hundred kids met at my house in the morning, and we marched in a parade to school all the way down Hyde Park Boulevard.

We all knew the words, and to the dismay of the night-shift workers in the neighborhood who were trying to sleep, we belted out the lyrics about a mighty lion in a peaceful village in the jungle.

The chorus grew louder as we approached Gaskill. When we got to the front of our school, Mark's brother Steve hoisted me up onto his shoulders as we sang and marched around the school. Penny and her team were marching in from the other direction. Drivers in cars beeped their horns. We felt invincible as we entered the gym for the rally. We couldn't have timed our entrance any better as our choir sang about hushing my darling. No one knew then, or until now, who I considered to be my darling. I even would have carried her books to school if she didn't live so far away.

After the rally in the gym, we moved to the auditorium for final speeches by the candidates. I was mesmerized by Penny's speech that day. I would have voted for her for President of the United States if I could have. As I got up to give my speech, I saw my mom in the back of the auditorium. I'm not sure parents were really allowed to be there, but once I saw her, I decided to give it my best. Mouths were watering in that auditorium as I described sixty-four flavors of ice cream in a way that swayed some of the undecided voters. I noticed my classmates Ben and Jerry taking careful notes. (They later moved to Vermont.)

When it was all over, we all went to our homerooms to place our votes. The Student Council officers counted them all day long.

And then it happened ...

Around 2 p.m. that afternoon, an announcement came over the loudspeaker. I was elected Student Council President, and Roberta was elected Vice President. Penny would be our Secretary and Sally Viverito would be our Treasurer. A few minutes after the announcement was made, the door to my homeroom opened. There was Penny with a big smile on her face. I rose to greet her. She held out her hand and said, "Congratulations Bob!" What a class act! I wanted to kiss her right on the lips, but everyone was looking at us, and I knew I hadn't the right to be so forward.

I never did get to carry Penny's books. I fell in love with another classmate at our election celebration party that evening. Such is junior high school romance. The whole next year we four served together on behalf of our classmates. We had a great time. My sister, Gloria, gave me a wood gavel when I won the election and I used it to open every meeting, but I always asked the other officers to use the gavel to close the meeting. By the end of the year, we had raised a lot of extra money from selling pizza and donuts at school dances and decided to leave the school a gift. If you happen to drive down Hyde Park Boulevard, take a look at the clock in the middle of five windows above the front door of Gaskill Middle School. That was Penny's idea.

In retrospect, I don't know how I won that election. I voted for Penny.

Twin Sisters and the Guys Who Marry Them

I am focusing today on one of life's greatest mysteries, and the small, exclusive group of guys who have figured it out. That's right, I'm talking about a guy who asks one of a pair of twin sisters for a date, and maybe even marries her.

These guys are my personal heroes, right up there, almost, with police officers, firefighters, and members of the armed forces. Well, maybe not that high, but I do think these guys are very clever, courageous, and under-appreciated. They are definitely higher on my list than cowards like me who would only ask a non-twin for a date.

To understand the infinite contours of this situation, you first need to understand where twin sisters come from. Let me explain. A lot of people don't know this but one of the prime causes of twins is the drinking water that comes from Niagara Falls. It's true. I have first-hand evidence. I checked the birth records at Niagara Falls Memorial Hospital and St. Mary's Hospital in Lewiston and cross-referenced those records against the Niagara Falls Water Department records and personal water drinking diaries of the moms in question and the facts are irrefutable.

The records clearly show that Mrs. Mariani, Mrs. Wade, Mrs. Scaletta and Mrs. Pullano each enjoyed a glass of Niagara Falls drinking water almost exactly nine months before giving birth to the most beautiful twin baby girls you can imagine. I'm no scientist but I'm pretty sure it has something to do with hydrogen. There are two hydrogen atoms for every oxygen atom in every molecule of water after all. So, the math clearly works out.

Now, to be clear, the science doesn't support the same conclusion for twin boys. The water records don't support the conclusion on the maternal side of these boy twins, but there is an interesting correlation on the paternal side with certain sales data from Carling's Black Label beer.

But I have meandered far from my original point, which is, how do guys ask a twin girl for a date? How does this happen? What was their plan? Was it intentional or happenstance? Did they take a class? I would love to know!

There are more possible moves in a chess game than there are atoms in the universe, yet this pales in comparison to the complexities involved in asking one of two twin sisters out on a date. And if you think you want to ask one twin for a date, you had better be really sure, because a golden rule of twindom is that there is no going back and asking the other one out if the first date fizzles. (I don't really know if this is true, but it should be a federal law.) There are probably other rules too, but none they teach you in school. So, you are totally on your own to figure this out.

I met my first twin from the opposite sex in kindergarten. Michele was sweet and pretty, and we are still friends more than a half century later. Of course, I didn't know she was a twin when we were in Mrs. Brown's class together. Her sister, Marcia, was imprisoned in another kindergarten class down the hall for most of the day, but it could have been in another city. "Down the hall" is a long way away for a kindergartener. I think the principal put them in separate classes because the teachers couldn't tell them apart, but nobody warned us kids.

At first, I didn't think Michele liked me much. I would say, "Hi Michele," at recess and she would look me square in the eyes and say, "I'm Marcia," in a way that made me know she knew who she was, and I didn't. I was worried about her at first, but she seemed to recover and know her real name once recess was over. It took a lot of courage just to talk to a girl in kindergarten and I resolved to learn all the girls' names before I ever addressed them again.

Encountering a set of twins for the first time can be unsettling for a little kid. I still vividly remember the first time the boys and girls in my class saw the Mariani twins walking down the hall at Hyde Park Elementary together, side by side. We froze in place, jaws dropped, mouths wide open. We parted the hallway for their processional like when Moses parted the Red Sea. We looked skyward for angels dropping twins from heaven. Theodore took off his glasses and polished them right on the spot, Timothy ran up behind them to look for trick carnival mirrors, and I personally called the school nurse to report the situation. It was mind-numbing and made all the more perplexing because their mom somehow thought it would be a good idea for them to wear the same dresses to school that day. Truth be told we boys had crushes on both of them all through elementary school but were too afraid to talk to either one for fear of saying the wrong name.

Think about it - what if you walked Michele home from school and fell in love with Marcia along the way? They lived in the same house after all. Think of the complications! What if you fell in love with both of them? Was that even possible? What if you went on a first date with Marcia and thought you were on a second date with her, but it was really Michele? What if you were talking to Michele on the phone, asked her if you could carry her books to school, and then heard Marcia giggle and hand the phone to her sister saying, "It's for you – some boy wants to carry your books." Oh, the red-faced possibilities! These were heady questions for a kid who just learned how to tie his shoelaces and write in cursive.

It's not that any of us were dating yet at that age, but we were cub scouts thinking ahead.

It didn't get any easier in junior high for twin-phobic boys like me. It turns out the elementary schools were twin-girl feeder systems for the junior high. The moms from 22nd Street School, 24th Street School, and 39th Street School all drank Niagara Falls water too! And it must have been flavored with Perrier, because all of these twins were drop-dead gorgeous. All of a sudden Carol and Cathy and Mary and Kathy joined Michele and Marcia. I had just figured out who was who between Ken and Keith on account of Ken broke his leg and Keith didn't when the twin girls overran the school. Forget about algebra – just keeping track of all these twins and their names was a math, spelling, and facial recognition challenge all in one.

Parents of twin girls don't help a fellow out much. They think it's funny to start the first name of each twin with the same letter. It's not enough to just dress them the same – right? We need more mystery and confusion.

I always liked Mary and Kathy Wade, and not just because their parents broke from tradition and gave them first names with different first letters. They were two of the few twins I could tell apart – for a while. Mary was serene, erudite and calming with a Mona Lisa smile; Kathy was bubbly with an easy laugh and sparkle in her eyes; both were pretty, smart, and nice. My friends and I devised a plan – we would have crushes on Kathy on Tuesdays and Thursdays and on Mary on Mondays and Wednesdays. Friday would be a day of rest, when we would study questions like why Cathy Scaletta's first name started with a "C" while Kathy Wade's first name started with a "K"?

Well, we boys weren't any smarter by the time we got to high school (just ask our female classmates). Our biggest fear was offending one twin by asking the other for a date to the school dance. We sweated profusely about this quandary, notwithstanding the fact that at every school dance I ever attended most of the boys stood with their guy friends on one side of the gym and the girls did the same on the other side. Only "Color my World" or "Stairway to Heaven" could bring us together.

And then it happened …

I was finally on a first name basis with Marcia and Michele, Mary and Kathy, Carol and Cathy, and could actually tell them all apart and spell all their names, when walking down the high school hallway in 10th grade came the Pullano twins, Anna and Rosa! It turned out that there were two more twin-girl feeder junior high schools in the city I didn't even know about! I now knew what higher mathematics was useful for. Now Anna and Rosa's mom definitely enjoyed Perrier – these twins were (and are) beautiful inside and out. It wasn't easy to tell them apart in high school at first, even with the powers I gained studying calculus and differential equations. At least their names didn't start with the same letter – that was helpful. There were only eight letters between them and three "As" among them! I never met their mom, but I loved her economical, melodious use of the alphabet. You could say Anna's name backwards and still get it right – that made a 10th grader happy – unless, of course, you were talking to Rosa. I sensed a love of animals and exclamation points in both of these sweet girls – they never met a stray puppy they didn't want to adopt or a sentence that couldn't use a few more exclamation points, but college came calling before the question of who was who could be resolved.

Before I close, I want to make it crystal clear that I've known enough beautiful twins to know that each one of the pairs is special in her own right. And I know that it doesn't take all that long to fully appreciate that for an adult, although it is above the pay grade of a typical fifth grader. But that doesn't diminish the strategic planning and obstacles encountered by would-be twin suitors. And it doesn't matter at all if one of these suitors is himself a twin – this gives him no real advantage! I suspect, but don't know for sure, that if a guy messes up with one twin, he messes up with her sister too! Think about that!

And so, my friends, I hope you'll join me in congratulating those lucky, smart, clever and courageous guys who figured out how to ask all these beautiful ladies for dates. Perhaps you've never thought about this question before (I never did until I had an hour to kill while inside my car while my wife was shopping at the Galleria Mall) but you have to marvel at how these guys could navigate the twindom sea of mysteries. And that was before the website, www.howtoaskonetwinsisterforadatewithoutoffending hersister.com was created!

So raise a glass to the most beautiful twins in the world – Marcia and Michele, Kathy and Mary, Carol and Cathy, and Anna and Rosa!

Kathy & Mary?

Marcia & Michele?   *Anna & Rosa?*

Crossin' the Crick
Without Permission

At precisely 6:31 p.m. on a cold winter Friday evening in 1970, I left my house at 2407 Niagara Avenue, for a long brisk walk down 24th Street. It was a ritual. I did this every Friday evening once I grew a moustache onto my fourteen-year-old face. As I crossed 24th Street at Grand Avenue and headed toward 22nd Street, I looked at my watch – right on time! I double-checked my pocket and there it was – one dollar and one penny.

At precisely 6:47 p.m. on that same cold winter night, my best friend Dan left his house at 534 27th Street heading out into the cold towards Pine Avenue. He took a left turn on Pine, heading for 22nd. He double-checked his pocket and there it was – one dollar and one penny.

We met at 7:00 p.m. at the deli at 22nd and Grand. Dan waited for me on the side of the building. He didn't dare walk in front of the store. He couldn't. He had a baby face. He didn't look like he was eighteen years old. He didn't even look fourteen. Dan handed me his one dollar and one penny.

I'm not sure how bank robbers feel before a big heist, but I can tell you that walking into a store when you are only fourteen years old to buy a six-pack of Molson Golden with exactly two dollars and two pennies, wearing only a moustache and carrying a fake ID from Reno, Nevada that you bought with a post office money order for three dollars from your paper route money through an ad you saw in Popular Electronics, is both exhilarating and nerve-wracking at the same time.

The cashier must have known. But he must have needed the money. He never questioned me. He just smiled as he rang up the six-pack and I handed him my two one-dollar bills and two pennies. Week after week he just smiled. I wonder if he knew my moustache was real – sideburns too! I wonder if he laughed as he pondered a couple of teenagers drinking a cold beer on an even colder winter night.

Dan gave me a high-five as I handed him a Molson and we headed to 24th Street School between Forest and Independence Avenues. We would sit on a bench in the first-base dugout adjacent the baseball diamond and sip our beer and ponder the world through our teenage eyes. We would talk about girls and football and school. We would talk about how great our junior high teachers were. We would talk a lot about what we wanted to do with the rest of our lives. Dan's dad had passed away a couple of years earlier, and he told me he was saving all of his survivor benefits to pay for dental school. I told him I was going to be an electrical engineer, if I didn't electrocute myself taking stuff apart before I got to college.

As we opened our last bottle we started our walk toward Hyde Park, headed for the ice-skating rink. We weren't going to the rink to skate. We were going to meet girls – we hoped! That's why we drank the beer – we might actually get the chance to talk to one!

We crossed the boulevard in front of the junior high school and waved to Lady Liberty on the other side. Gill Creek was frozen over – it always was in January. So, we would cross it and slip-slide over to the other side. We were talking and laughing as we got to the middle of the creek.

And then it happened …

From both sides of the creek – from both banks – bright spotlights suddenly blinded us from all directions. Someone with authority bellowed through a bullhorn:

"This is the police! Slowly walk to the bank. Don't run. You can't escape!"

I don't mind saying now that I was scared sh!tless then. I looked at Dan and he looked at me. We were both plastered and confused. Dan calmly said, "Seems a bit extreme for six bottles of beer."

The spotlights followed us like dancers on a stage as we made our way to the opposing bank. Two officers grabbed our arms and walked us to their car. We were shivering from the cold and even more from fright. We quietly wondered if we would be arrested, incarcerated, and kicked out of the National Junior Honor Society. The officers ushered us into the backseat and started the interrogation.

"What were you doing in the middle of the creek?"

"We were walking," I quickly replied. I decided I would answer all the easy questions and leave the hard ones for Dan.

"Where were you going?"

"To the ice rink."

"Where are your skates?"

"We don't skate."

"Then why were you going to the ice rink?"

"To maybe meet girls."

One of the officers tried to hide his chuckle as he followed up, "You guys smell like a Genesee Brewery!"

"It's Molson Golden," I replied. Dan and I had a reputation to protect. If our names got into the newspaper, I wanted everyone to know that it was imported beer.

"Where did you get the beer?"

"From my parents' fridge," I lied.

"You don't seem old enough to be drinking beer. Why are you drinking?"

"I told you - because we might have to talk to girls later."

I think the officers were really having a fun time with this little question and answer session, so they continued.

"What were you doing before you reached the creek?"

"I was explaining Ohm's law and Kirchoff's law of electrical circuits to Dan, and he was explaining how an oral surgeon does a root canal to me," I replied. If we were going to jail for drinking beer, I at least wanted them to know that we were both on the honor roll.

It was then that they decided they had heard enough and drove us to the police station for further questioning. They asked us to empty our pockets before taking us into a room with lights way too bright for a kid who had just imbibed three bottles of beer. Then they separated us and asked us both a whole new round of questions. We were there for an hour when I had had enough.

"Are you arresting us or not?" I asked, as Dan wondered too.

The officer showed us his clipboard where he had written down his notes. There it was, right at the top, in big bold printed letters, "Crossin the crick without permission".

"Is that what we are being charged with? Crossing the creek?" I asked.

"Maybe."

"You should fix the spelling. You misspelled 'creek'."

"Are you some kind of smart-ass!"

"I am smart, but I am not an ass. I'm just trying to help you with your spelling in case you want to become a detective someday."

It was then that he asked if I wanted him to call my parents to come and pick me up. I begged him not to. He asked Dan too. Dan told him that he didn't have a father so he would have to call his mother, but he wished he wouldn't.

And then it happened …

The captain entered the room and told us that we were "free to go". Those are the best three words a kid can hear from a police officer, a school principal, or a judge. The captain told the officer that he was sure we didn't do it.

"Do what?"

"Boys, somebody poured gasoline on the snow fence in the park tonight and lit it ablaze. It was a stupid and dangerous thing to do. We just caught him."

Dan and I continued to meet up just about every Friday night for the next eight years. More times than not we shared a Molson Golden. We even got to talk to girls and even hold their hands and steal some kisses. We never crossed the creek without permission again.

Dan crossed the bridge to heaven a month after he

started dental school, almost eight years after we crossed the creek without permission. I think about him often, and always on Friday evenings around 7 p.m. I always carry a single dollar bill and a single penny in my pocket too. I only drink one beer a week now, and even that makes me sleepy. Before I take a sip, I close my eyes, picture him standing outside the deli at 22nd and Grand with his one dollar and one penny, and then raise my glass. I know he is raising his too.

It's a Small World!

It was the 254th day of the year 1983. It was an unusually warm September Sunday even for Cincinnati. I started my day in my apartment in Fort Mitchell, Kentucky with a cup of coffee while my rescue cat Mitchell sipped from a bowl of milk at my feet. I read the paper and wrote a love letter to a girl back in Buffalo who I hoped to marry someday. I went to my closet and picked out some "neutral" casual clothes. Most of these clothes I picked out myself. Most of these clothes would be donated to Goodwill shortly after I said, "I do!"

I couldn't wear what I really wanted to wear. I couldn't wear my Buffalo Bills jersey and cap. This would be my first Bills-Bengals game after all. I'd be in the stands at Riverfront Stadium with my dear friends. They would all be wearing Bengals' attire, and they would protect me if they had to, but I didn't want them to have to. All my friends called me "Buffalo Bob" and they knew about my allegiance to the Bills. They loved me anyway.

It reached 94 degrees during that game on September 11, 1983. It was a scorcher. Joe Ferguson threw a 14-yard touchdown pass that day. Joe Cribbs played a great game. I remember Ken Anderson quarterbacking for the Bengals and Cris Collinsworth catching his passes. It was a low-scoring game, lots of three-downs and out. Lots of punting.

My friends and I were seated about mid-way up on the 35-yard line on the home team side of the stadium. My friends were all to the right of me and a girl of about fourteen was just to my left, and her dad was just to her left.

I didn't cheer when the Bills scored that day, nor did I cheer when the Bengals scored. I left that to my friends.

And then it happened ...

I noticed that this sweet teenage girl sitting next to me didn't cheer when the Bills made a first down or even when they scored. But she didn't cheer for the Bengals either. I caught her smiling at her dad and him smiling back whenever the Bills did something good. It was one of those precious exchanges between a father and daughter that I could only dream about back then and have come to treasure now.

It was in the fourth quarter when I asked her, "Are you a Buffalo Bills fan?" I whispered.

She looked to her dad for permission. "It's OK," he nodded, "you can tell him."

"Yes, how did you guess?"

"You didn't cheer when the Bengals scored, but you smiled at your dad when the Bills scored. You smiled just like me!"

"Are you a Bills' fan too?" she asked.

"Yes, I am. In fact, I'm from Niagara Falls, New York."

"You're kidding! Me too."

"Really? Well, I lived on Niagara Avenue near 24th Street growing up."

"You're kidding! We live on Niagara Avenue near 22nd Street right now!"

And so, it was. We were but two of 46,839 people in the stands that day. What are the odds that two Buffalo Bills fans who once lived within a single city block of one another in Niagara Falls would end up sitting right next to each other to watch the Bills beat the Bengals 10-6 in Riverfront Stadium on a hot September day in Cincinnati?

I married that Buffalo girl I wrote the love letter to on that September Sunday morning. It turns out that she knows football better than I do. Her dad took her to see the Buffalo Bills play at the old War Memorial Stadium. He explained the game to her when she was just a young girl. I wonder if they exchanged special daddy-daughter smiles when the Bills scored. Now she has an uncanny ability to announce the gameday penalties before the officials do!

As for those Northern Kentucky friends and Bengals fans, most of them came to my wedding. One of them, Phil, was one of my groomsmen. We exchanged text messages during the Bills' playoff game last month, and again during the Bengals games. I'll be rooting for the Bengals on Super Bowl Sunday. That's what friends do. But I will be wearing my Bills jersey and cap. That's what Bills' Mafia does. And Ellen will be wearing her Bills apparel too!

"Go Bengals!"

"Go Bills!"

The Jigsaw and the Girl Scout Cookies

Sometimes a guy can only take so much sitting at his desk practicing law, putting stamps into his album, or watching a game on television. Every once in a while, a guy has to prove that he is a guy, and to do this he needs to fix something, build something, or install something. Every guy worth his salt knows this feeling. It is an itch that needs to be scratched. I imagine, but don't know for sure, that this itch is about half as strong as the itch my wife and daughter feel just before they decide to go shopping.

And so, it was this past Saturday morning when I decided I needed to install an electrical outlet in my mancave. I have fourteen outlets already, but a proper mancave needs fifteen. I needed this outlet, hidden behind a chest, so that I could power a Philips Hue White and Color Ambiance Beyond LED Dimmable Smart Table Lamp with 16 million colors all controllable from my iPhone X. I have been planning where to place this lamp in my mancave for months. I've drawn 3D models of the lamp sitting atop the chest with my AutoCad software. I've measured everything out to the millimeter. It's a big deal to me, on account of I am only allowed to make interior design decisions in one room in our house – that room being my cave. That was the deal – I agree to move into my mother-in-law's house, and I get to decorate my cave without female intervention.

I am an electrical engineer, and I worked as an electrician's helper at a power plant one semester in college. I have a Craftsman six-drawer super deluxe toolbox on heavy duty casters loaded to the brim with every imaginable tool. Some of those tools I've even actually used. I know I could probably cut the rectangular hole in the drywall for the outlet with a hand tool. But hand tools are for amateurs. This job calls for an electric jigsaw. I know I own one. I bought it on July 8, 1992, which is the last time I decided to pretend I was a contractor. But I can't find it. It is not in the drawer where I kept my circular saw, reciprocating saw, and chain saw. They are all missing!

"Honey, have you seen my Black & Decker jigsaw?" I yell up the stairs.

"Your what?"

I love my wife, but she is useless when it comes to helping me find my lost tools.

But it's no matter. Part of the ritual of doing a home construction project is the trip to Ed Young's Hardware

Store to buy the tools and supplies. I changed out of my dress slacks, button-down Oxford shirt and sport coat, and put on a pair of jeans, a flannel shirt, a tool belt, and tucked a pencil over my ear to venture out. I even rubbed some dirt on my jeans. Image is everything for a guy in a hardware store. Guys like me, who push pencils during the week, and hit our fingers with hammers on weekends, like to strut into the hardware store like Mr. Fix-it. We all sit in our cars Googling terms like float valve, ground fault interrupter, bushing, and flux. We are weekend warriors. We don't do this every day. But it's important that we walk the walk and talk the talk. It's a macho thing. I marched through the front door of Ed Young's store with a swagger.

And then it happened …

There they were – just past the springtime offerings of gas grilles that my wife won't let me buy. Six of the cutest girl scouts in Williamsville, standing behind a six-foot-long table loaded with boxes of Girl Scout cookies. I had barely opened the store door when the girls sang out in perfect harmony and excitement, "Mister – would you like to buy a box of Girl Scout cookies?"

They were Daisies, Brownies, Junior Girl Scouts, Cadette Girl Scouts and Senior Girl Scouts. They were arranged side by side in ascending order of height from right to left. They had each won merit badges in cuteness and sweetness. They were innocent and hopeful, one and all, trusting in the hope and optimism of children, that adults would stop and help their cause. And how could you not. I stopped dead in my tracks and soaked in their beautiful smiles and looks of anticipation. They awaited my answer as their beaming moms stood nearby. I really didn't need to answer out loud for the moms. They knew they had hooked a dad with a daughter, albeit fully grown. Once a dad, always a dad.

"Well, of course, I'd be happy to buy some cookies! But there are six of you – who should I buy my cookies from?"

Six hands attached to six arms shot up before my question was even finished. The youngest two were hopping up and down hoping to be noticed. Each girl was as cute as the next. I glanced at the moms as I fell into this beautifully laid trap. It was marketing at its finest. I knew then what I have always suspected – women are smarter than men! No decent man can turn down a request to buy Thin Mints or Shortbread cookies from a Girl Scout in a hardware store.

So, one by one, I took a box of cookies from the stack in front of each girl. They couldn't believe it. I could see it in their eyes. This old guy with gray hair must be a millionaire. Nobody buys this many boxes of cookies. He must have won the lottery. They giggled, smiled, and laughed all at once. Their moms smiled too. Nothing warms the heart of a mom quite so much as someone showing their daughters that there is goodness in this world. I imagined they just might have a story to tell on their way home from the store that afternoon and tell a story they should. They made my day.

A small crowd had gathered as our transaction was coming to a close. I reached for my wallet and gave them a look. I could tell they were wondering if I had enough money to actually pay for the cookies.

"Wait a minute. How much money do I owe you?"

The Senior Scout knew but I signaled for her to shush.

"Who is the youngest scout here?"

A Daisy kindergartener with a brunette Bob cut raised her hand, proudly but timidly.

"How much do I owe you, Miss?"

She squirmed and smiled as I glanced at the price list on the easel. Her colleagues figured out the total before she did and wanted to whisper in her ear, but to their credit they gave her a chance. You could just see her trying to figure out if she should add or multiply. The grandmothers in the crowd shouted encouragement, but I sensed some of the grandfathers were holding up fingers. But she paid no attention. She was going to solve this math problem all on her own. After ten agonizing seconds that seemed a lot longer, she asked me if I owed her $30. Never before was such applause heard in Ed

Young's Hardware Store on a Saturday afternoon.

I reached into my wallet and handed the Senior Scout two twenty-dollar bills. She thanked me and then asked me, "Would you like any change?" I am seldom left speechless by a fourteen-year-old, but speechless I was. The moms were roaring with laughter. I glanced their way. This Senior Scout watches online MBA courses from the Wharton School of Business.

"Ladies, I do need a few dollars in change to buy a jigsaw please."

The young ladies boxed up my cookies and promised to keep them safe for me as I did my shopping. I could still hear them laughing as I picked out my jigsaw and headed for the electrical department. A grandmother in the checkout line flashed me a smile as I headed back to the cookie display.

My wife greeted me in the kitchen as I unloaded my boxes of Thin Mints and Shortbread cookies. "I thought you went to the hardware store?"

"Girl Scouts."

Ellen smiled.

I went shopping for a jigsaw and came home with a smile. I poured a glass of milk and broke open the Thin Mints. Next Saturday I might just cut a hole in a wall.

Thank You Harold Burns!

It was a hot sunny day in July in Niagara Falls. It was Thursday, July 20, 1939, to be exact. Young Lenny's favorite team, the New York Yankees, led by Joe DiMaggio, Bill Dickey and Lefty Gomez, were playing the St. Louis Browns in an away game. He could have listened to the game on the radio, but Len and his buddies from Niagara and Cleveland Avenues had other plans.

There were apples to be eaten, a lake to be swum in, and girls to impress. So off they went on their bicycles, down Hyde Park Boulevard to the river, down Lewiston hill, heading north towards the lake and the famous apple orchards of Niagara County. The apples weren't ready for picking yet, of course. The McIntosh apples wouldn't be ready for picking until late August or September, but that didn't deter the Niagara Falls youngsters. Unripe apples in these famous orchards are bitter, not sour, and you could prove your manhood to your friends by picking them without getting caught and eating them without getting sick.

I'm not sure how many green apples young Lenny ate

that day, but I am sure it was too many. I'm sure he worked up quite a sweat on that long bike ride from Niagara Falls to Wilson – I know, I've done it a few times myself. He must have been sweltering when he made the near life-ending decision to enter the waters of Lake Ontario at Wilson Beach on that beautiful afternoon.

Len was eighteen years old, but he wasn't a strong swimmer. Baseball was his sport. His young friend, Russell, was only thirteen, and lived a couple of houses away from Len on Niagara Avenue. Russell Irwin was a good kid, the kind of kid who would do anything for you, so the older kids in the neighborhood never minded when he tagged along, even if they had to wait for him to catch up as they pedaled their bikes down the old Ridge Road.

That cool water must have felt great on that hot summer day as Len jumped in and started swimming for Canada. A young girl's float had gotten away from her at the beach and the wind and currents were carrying it away. Len heard her cry and decided to help. He kicked and swam as hard as he could, but the float kept drifting further and further out. It must have been about 100 yards from shore.

And then it happened …

The green apple cramps started slowly but worsened quickly. Before he knew it, Len was in excruciating pain.

His body curled up in a ball in the lake. He couldn't kick his legs. He couldn't swim. He couldn't even do the doggie paddle. He gasped for air as he struggled to stay afloat. He went under and then bobbed above the surface. The little girl screamed. Lenny was drowning.

Russell Irwin didn't think twice. He bolted to the water's edge and jumped in. He swam as hard and as fast as he could to get to his friend. He reached him first but was too small to save him. He went under himself. He struggled nonetheless, risking his own young life to save his friend.

And then it happened …

As a crowd of worried onlookers gathered on the beach, Harold Burns, son of World War I veteran Cornelius Burns, of 2942 Cleveland Avenue, just seventeen years old himself, swam faster than he ever had in his life. He grabbed unconscious Lenny under one arm, and then swam and kicked all the way to shore. Russell struggled to keep up with him. Together they dragged Lenny onto the beach and laid him out spread eagle on his back on the warm sand. Moms and dads and daughters and sons looked on. Some cried. But Harold wasn't done. He opened Lenny's mouth, pressed on his chest, and pushed out the water from the mighty lake. He knelt down and gave Lenny a kiss of life. Then he blew his own breath into Lenny's lungs. In those days they called it "artificial respiration". On any day they call it saving a life.

For two long minutes Harold tried to revive his neighborhood friend. How tired he must have been. How scared he must have been. How determined he must have been.

And then it happened ...

Five minutes after losing consciousness, Lenny coughed. It wasn't much of a cough, not the kind of cough that a person would be proud of. But it was the kind that tells a bunch of worried folks on a beach that you are alive. And then he coughed and coughed and coughed. He spit out the water from Lake Ontario. And

then he opened his eyes to see Russell Irwin looking down at him, with Harold Burns standing behind Russell.

"What's going on Russell?"

"You drowned Lenny! But Harold and I saved you! Harold even kissed you!"

"He kissed me? Oh shit! Promise me fellas - no one tells our parents!"

"We promise!"

But the boys couldn't keep their secret. It's hard to keep secret the saving of a life. Witnesses to the heroic act talked about it for weeks. Niagara Falls is a small town. Everybody knows everybody. The story made it to the front page of the Niagara Falls Gazette on Thursday, July 27, 1939. It also came to the attention of the local American Legion Post, where Harold Burns' father was a member. They wanted to give him a medal.

Harold didn't get in trouble for stealing those apples. Neither did Russell or Lenny. I don't know if Harold received his medal, but I hope he did. I hope Russell got one too.

I never met Harold Burns. I've been trying to track down his family. I want to say thank you to his children and grandchildren. I wonder if he knew that Lenny would never have met the love of his life, Blanche Stella Duff, of New Bedford, Massachusetts, but for him. I wonder if he knew that there were four kids who grew up on Niagara Avenue in Niagara Falls that

POWER CITY OF THE WORLD-NEW YORK STATE'S TENTH CITY

NIAGARA FALLS GAZETTE Home Edition

THIRTY-FOUR PAGES   NIAGARA FALLS, N. Y., THURSDAY, JULY 27, 1939   THIRTY-FOUR PAGES   PRICE THREE CENTS

SEEK HERO AWARD FOR FALLS YOUTH

Efforts on the part of American Legion officials to get a hero medal for Harold Burns, 17 years old, 2942 Cleveland Avenue, today brought to light his participation in the rescue, at Wilson's beach on Lake Ontario last Thursday, of Len Simpson, 18 years old, 2216 Niagara Avenue. Also participating in the Rescue was Russell Irwin, 13 years old, 2206 Niagara Avenue.

According to witnesses of the incident Simpson was stricken with a cramp while swimming to a float some distance off shore at the beach and sand. Noting his plight, young Irwin, himself not a good swimmer, dived in and attempted to save Simpson but was pulled under the surface of the water and had to give up his effort.

Burns, who was on the beach at the time, then went to the rescue and brought Simpson to shore in an unconscious condition. He applied artificial respiration and Simpson recovered within five minutes and was taken to his home. Because of their fear of parental reprimand, the three young men decided to keep the incident a secret but Legion officials learned of the rescue from witnesses and are at present investigating with the end in view of obtaining a medal for Burns.

never would have, but for him. That's right, I wouldn't be here but for Harold. My daughter wouldn't be here either. I wonder if Harold knew that Staff Sergeant Lenny wouldn't have served his country in England, France, and Germany in World War II, but for him.

I wonder if he is looking down now and reading these words and smiling because he is not forgotten. I wonder if he remembers saving my father, Leonard P. Simpson, from drowning in Lake Ontario on that hot summer day in July 1939.

My father never talked much about almost drowning. When he did, he just mumbled something about "rotten apples". We know he was always grateful to Harold and Russell.

Thank you, Harold Burns and Russell Irwin.

Single Sugar, Double Cream

He awoke every morning at 5:30 a.m. and tip-toed through the house from the bedroom to the kitchen, being careful not to wake my mom, my baby brother or my two sisters. He did this every workday for forty-five years. He thought we didn't hear him. He thought we didn't notice. But I heard him. I noticed. I heard the tea kettle whistle on the stove. It whistled for just a few seconds every morning at precisely 5:48 a.m. It was more reliable than a crowing rooster on a farm. He grabbed it quickly before it hit the high note and woke everybody up. He filled his coffee cup to an inch from the top. It was Maxwell House, the instant kind of coffee. He measured one teaspoon of sugar and filled the rest of the cup with milk. He stirred with one hand and smoked a cigarette with the other. He didn't eat breakfast – just one cup of coffee was all he needed.

And, just like that, he was gone. I jumped out of bed and watched him through my bedroom window. He got into his car and drove away. I didn't know where he went, but I knew he would come back home every day at 3:45 p.m.

I was only five when I got up the nerve. The sun was still sleeping. I waited under my blanket until I heard the whistle. Then I bolted from my warm bed and into my slippers and tip-toed like my dad past my parents' bedroom. I snuck into the living room and peered around the corner into the kitchen. It was then that he caught me. My dad held his index finger to his lips to shush me, and then motioned with that finger to come to him.

"What are you doing up so early?" he whispered.

"I heard you dad, and I wanted to know what you do in the kitchen every morning, and where you go so early every day."

"I go to the plant. I work to make money to put a roof over our heads and food on the table," he explained.

"What's in the cup dad?"

"It's coffee. Would you like a sip?"

I was too young to drink coffee, and he knew it. He made me promise not to tell my mom. It was only a small sip but a big secret between father and son.

It was a delicious secret, and one I've cherished for all these years. I didn't always join him at the kitchen table in the early morning, but by the time I was six my dad had explained to me what he did at the plant. He "measured carbon." He was a "quality control inspector." He taught those "college kids" how to do things the right way. He taught them not to goof off and how to work hard. And I believed him. He had been in the army after all. And there was nothing that he couldn't do.

And then it happened …

I was almost seven years old when I heard the whistle and joined my dad at the table. To my great surprise that Friday morning, there were two cups on the table.

"What's this, dad?"

"You've got a big test in school today son. Drink up and you'll do fine!"

And then he shared his secret recipe with me …

"Single sugar, double cream!" he told me, "Caramel color is best. Not enough cream or too much sugar and you'll be jumpy all day! Coffee one inch from the top. Stir the sugar before you add the cream. You've got to make it right the first time, and then don't touch it until it's gone!"

From that day 'til now I've taken more tests than I can remember. I've taken pop quizzes, mid-terms and final

exams, multiple choice, true-false, essays and fill-in-the-blanks. It makes no difference to me. I've taken attorney bar exams in four jurisdictions. I enjoyed the Florida Bar Exam so much that I took it twice. And every test day, and every other day, has started the same, with the same cup of coffee my dad showed me how to make when I was seven. We didn't tell my mom until I was sixteen!

My wife and I go out to breakfast together every Sunday morning. The server at our favorite spot brings our coffee cups to the table just the way I like it – one inch from the top. I carefully measure one teaspoon of sugar and stir, then add a double-cream. When my cup is half empty the server rushes over and offers a warm-up. I cover my cup with my hand. My wife just smiles. The server seems puzzled.

"Single sugar – double cream. Don't touch it until it's gone," I explain. She smiles and I leave her a big tip.

Every day is a test. And caramel color is best.

My dad worked as a quality control inspector at Union Carbide on Hyde Park Boulevard in Niagara Falls for more than forty-five years. He left our home every morning at 6:30 a.m. He never woke my mom on his way to the kitchen. His workday started at 7:00 a.m. and it was only a five-minute car ride. But he was never late for work. He always called it "the plant." He told me many times over dinner how he showed some college kid how to do his job. He told me this so often that I was afraid to tell him I had decided to go to college after high school. He just smiled and told me to bring my tough homework problems to him and he would show me the ropes. I'm pretty sure he was very proud when I graduated from college. But he told me I was a flaming nutcase for giving up a good engineering job to go to law school.

"Single sugar – double cream," I told him.

Little League Lessons
(My Dad Taught Me How to Catch)

When I was ten years old, I waited on the top step of my front porch every summer day for my dad to come home from work. He parked his blue Ford Galaxie 500 in front of our house every afternoon at 3:30 p.m. on the dot, climbed the porch steps, tapped me atop my head and told me, "Get ready!" He went inside, handed his lunch box to my mom and gave her a big kiss smack on the lips. My mom was always standing tall at the kitchen stove stirring, cooking, and baking, before she shooed him away. "Go on – he's been waiting for you for an hour!"

And so it was, day after day, week after week, – our afternoon games of catch. My dad played catcher on an American Legion team when he was younger. He told me that hitting and throwing were important, but that, at my age, catching a baseball was the most important thing. He threw me line drives, pop flies and grounders. And my dad knew baseball. He saw Lou Gehrig play in person when the Yankees played the Indians in Cleveland. He knew every player on the Yankees, at every position, in every season back to 1927. He knew most of their batting averages too. We would watch the Yankees play some of their home games on our General Electric 19" black and white TV on Saturdays and listen to most of their away games on my dad's six transistor radio.

The games came alive on the radio. I liked listening to games with my dad on the radio even more than I liked watching them on TV. You could just picture in your head what was happening on the field. "It's a hard-hit ball to Kubek at short. He's going to have to hurry to double up! He fields it cleanly, flips it over to Richardson at second. Are you kidding me! Bobby caught that ball barehanded and whipped it over to Joe Pepitone at first – just in time to turn two! Holy cow!"

"What happened dad?" "Didn't Bobby Richardson use his glove to catch that throw from Tony Kubek?" "Can you really catch a ball in your bare hand?"

"Yes, son, Bobby is a special player. Not too many guys could make that play like Bobby did, even in the big leagues. I told you, catching is a really important part of baseball. You can't throw it if you can't catch it first."

I learned just how important catching a baseball was when my dad came home from work one Thursday afternoon in the spring of my eleventh year. Until then my dad played catch barehanded with me, and he let me use his old American Legion team catcher's mitt. It was a funny mitt. It looked like a brown glazed donut with a hole in the middle that didn't go all the way through. You had to line up that hole with the ball dead on. If you didn't the ball would bounce off the outer ring of padding.

"Come with me," he said, as he gathered a shoebox full of S&H Green Stamps from under his bed. "We're going shopping!"

"For what?"

"A first baseman's glove!"

I couldn't believe it! My dad took me to Hens & Kelly department store. We headed straight for the sporting goods department. There were genuine major league baseballs and Louisville Slugger baseball bats on display. There were Spalding and Rawlings baseball gloves by the dozen, for every position on the field. My dad took me to the first baseman's gloves and told me to pick one out.

"Why first base dad?"

"Because you can catch!"

My dad spent $4.97 worth of S&H Green Stamps on that glove for me, almost all of the books in his shoebox, and it wasn't even my birthday! He even paid cash for a tin of Neatsfoot oil.

"Rub that Neatsfoot oil all over your glove tonight before you go to bed. Stick a baseball in your glove and tie it shut with shoelaces. That will get your glove used to the shape of the ball and help you to catch even better!"

I did exactly what my dad told me. Then I tucked the tied-up glove and ball under my blanket and fell off to dream about playing first base for the Yankees. If you've never enjoyed the smell of Neatsfoot oil rubbed into a new baseball glove, I can tell you that it is right up there with the smell of fresh-baked apple pie and pure vanilla extract. And it makes you dream of the big leagues!

But before I played first base for the Yankees, on the very next Saturday morning, I had to join all the other eleven-year-olds in my neighborhood for the North End Little League tryouts at Hyde Park. My friends and I were about to graduate from the Kiwanis League where we only got to wear matching T-shirts and caps that we bought with money from paper drives. This was the real Little League, with full uniforms and a chance to play in the Little League World Series in Williamsport, Pennsylvania.

My dad drove me to the tryouts which started at 10 a.m. sharp. He parked his car on Linwood Avenue and stood under a tree to watch us. It was a regular Little League draft day. We all had to stand in line to bat against twelve-year-old pitchers. Then they hit balls to us in the infield and outfield and watched us catch and throw. The team coaches all had clipboards with kids' names on them, and they graded us all on our baseball skills.

But a funny thing happened just before I took my place at first base, the position I wanted to play. A kid from the first-place team came up to me and asked if I would like to play on the best team in the league.

"Sure, I would!"

"Well, we need a first baseman, but we get the last pick in the draft. So, you need to make a bunch of errors in the field during your tryout. Catch a few, but make sure you miss as many as you catch."

I was confused. I set out that day to play the best baseball that I could. I set out to catch every ball hit my way. It didn't sound right to me that I should intentionally not catch the baseballs that came my way. I ran over to my dad standing under that tree.

"Dad – my friend just asked me to make a bunch of errors in the field, so I get drafted by the best team in the league. What should I do?"

"Son – I didn't buy you that glove for you to make errors. I think you know what you should do. And I think you know what Joe Pepitone would do."

And then it happened ...

I caught every ball they hit to me that day. I caught pop flies, line drives and hard-hit grounders. I caught errant throws from third base, shortstop and second base. I even caught some grounders back-handed just to show them that I could. I did my Neatsfoot-oiled, S&H Green Stamps-bought, Joe Pepitone-signed first baseman's glove proud! I did my dad proud too.

I didn't get drafted by the first-place team, or the second-place team, or the third-place team. I was drafted second in the first round by the Tavano Insurance Pirates, the team with the purple caps. The Pirates had finished second to last the year before. They were coached by Mr. Miller and Mr. Rodriguez. My friends Steve and Jim Miller played on that team. My friend, Greg Zipp, was drafted first by the last-place Mets, the team with the black caps. Greg was the best southpaw pitcher in the draft.

My team finished second to last place again that season, just ahead of the Mets. And it wasn't for lack of trying. I remember all of the fans clearing out of the third base bleachers when I came to the plate, on account of I always swung too early and pulled a ton of foul balls towards those bleachers. Once I almost hit Mrs. Miller in the face but she stuck up her glove just in time and caught a line drive before she scolded me and told me to never do that again! I remember the fans clearing out of the first base bleachers too, whenever my friend and teammate, Mark Aiduk, came to bat, on account of he always swung late. Some games the fans in the stands got more exercise than the players on the field!

And I remember that I caught every ball hit my way and every ball thrown my way that season. I even backhanded some. And I remember being selected as the starting first baseman on the North End Little League All-Star team that year. My friend Greg made the All-Star team too. We didn't make it to Williamsport, but we all had a great time.

It's funny though, what I remember most about my time in Little League wasn't my hits, throws or catches. It wasn't even making the All-Star team. What I remember most is looking up at my dad under a maple tree on Linwood Avenue on a sunny summer day and him telling me, "I think you know what you should do."

My dad taught me how to catch.

He taught me a few other things too.

The Coach's Whistle

[Whistle blows!]

Please take a knee.

As I've gotten older and the aches and pains of life catch up with me, I sometimes have a little trouble falling asleep at night. I start to think about the things I can't do anymore. It is then that I turn to one or two memories from my younger days. As I lay my head on my pillow, the memories come into my head. They always start with a familiar sound – the Coach's whistle!

I was nine years old in the fall of 1965. My oldest sister, Gloria, was dating Greg Brinda, the star halfback on the Niagara Falls High School Power Cats football team. The team practiced at Hyde Park, right across the street from my elementary school. It was a long way for a little kid to walk, but my mom let me go to the park every day after school to watch the team practice. I stood alone on the sideline day after day. I watched them throw and catch passes. I watched them do blocking and tackling drills. I ran along the sideline when they did their wind sprints at the end of each practice. I raced right alongside them.

At the end of one of those practices, Coach Cal blew his whistle. He told his team to "take a knee." He had a football in his hand. He walked over to me on the sideline. I was scared to death. When he got close, he bent over me and asked, "What's your name?"

"Robert Simpson."

"Simpson - do you like football?" (Coach Cal called everybody by their last name.)

"Yes."

"Can you catch?"

"Yes."

"Are you ready?"

"Yes."

Coach Cal backed up and threw me the football from about ten yards away. I caught it! He smiled. I got ready to throw it back when he held up his hand. "You keep it! Take it home with you. Walk with it. Run with it. And carry it back here to practice tomorrow." Well ... I carried that football everywhere. I ate breakfast and dinner with that football. I had it on my lap when I did my homework. I slept with it too. And, day after day, I brought that football to the high school practice field. This went on for weeks.

And then it happened ...

A few days before opening day, Coach Cal came over

to me again. He asked me if I wanted to be the official ball boy for the Niagara Falls High School Power Cats. "Sure," I said. I had no idea what a ball boy was.

"Great! Brinda will bring you to the team bus. See you on the sideline."

This was a big deal. I rode on the team bus with Chuck "Augie" Augustino, our quarterback, Greg Brinda, Joe Mauldin, Tom Buffamonte, Mike Gallina and Luciano Giampa. Don't those just sound like football names? I sat on the bus with Gerald Anthony DeMunda, a great guy who became a Marine and gave his life for our country in 1967 in Vietnam. Those guys treated me like a little brother. On opening day, they put black grease on my cheeks under my eyes. I don't think that grease did a darn thing, but the guys told me it would make me run faster.

I had an important job at the game. I brought water to the players and gave the referees clean footballs when they asked for one. After we kicked off and the referee blew the opening play dead, it was my job to run as fast as I could to the center of the field to retrieve the kicking tee. Sometimes Coach Cal would give me a high five if I ran really fast. I did this at all our home games, even the games played "under the lights" past my bedtime.

When the season ended, I tried to give my football back to Coach Cal. His reply, "Keep it kid – you earned it! Practice catching it and running with it and someday maybe you can play for the team!"

Fast forward eight years and I found myself on the same practice field with Coach Cal. I was a proud member of the Niagara Falls High School Power Cats.

Coach was a smart guy. He surrounded himself with talented and sometimes colorful assistant coaches. In my senior year, his assistants were Frank Scaletta, Chuck Sirianni and Roger Hailey. Defensive Coach Scaletta approached me in the first practice and asked me to try out for defensive back. He knew I was pretty fast. I lasted two plays on defense. I remember it like it was yesterday. I was playing cornerback. I was covering Michael Owens. I thought we were in a zone. I thought we were in a corner-rotation and I was supposed to blitz the quarterback.

We weren't.

Owens blew by me, caught a pass, and scored a touchdown during practice. Coach Scaletta came over to me. Big heart, great coach, but scary as hell to a seventeen-year-old. It went down like this ...

"Simpson, what the hell happened?"

"Well Coach, I thought ..."

"You THOUGHT? Who told you to think? Coaches think, players play! Stop listening to the peanut gallery and start playing football!"

I glanced to my right and there was Coach Cal, arms folded, whistle around his neck, grinning. It was at that moment that Coach Cal approached Coach Scaletta. They enjoyed a brief private conversation, and a minute later I became the starting wide receiver on the offense. Coach Cal saved me from the defense! It was clear to me and everyone else on the team that I sucked on defense, but Coach Cal never mentioned the blown play. He never mentioned what I couldn't do, he only told me what I could do – run fast and catch a football.

I loved my coach, and I loved to run.

As every Power Cat who played for Coach Cal knows, every practice ended the same way – with 100-yard wind sprints.

Coach Cal would blow his whistle near the end of every practice.

"Linemen – on the goal line!"

The tackles, guards, center and defensive linemen would all line up for the 100-yard sprint. They mostly hated this. They were big. They were strong. The ground shook like a buffalo stampede as they all ran down the field. I use the word "ran" loosely. These guys were really, really slow. Marty Shimmel, who really wasn't all that fast himself, could walk backward faster than these guys could run forward. We told jokes and smiled at the cheerleaders while they moseyed along. For linemen it was more like a Sunday stroll than a sprint. But they never knew how slow they really were, because Coach Cal was there every step of the way telling them how fast they were. And they believed him!

The linebackers, tight ends and quarterbacks ran

next. They were faster so we told shorter jokes.

At long last came the coach's whistle for the final group - the running backs, defensive backs and wide receivers. This was my group. Our sprints would determine the "fastest Cat" on the team. It always came down to the late Joel Barksdale and me.

I wasn't faster than Joel. He knew it and I knew it, but I never lost a race to him. He never lost to me either. The first time we had a wind sprint show-down, Joel lined up five yards to my left for our 100-yard dash. We exploded in a burst of speed when the coach blew his whistle. We were fully loaded down with shoulder pads, rubber spiked shoes and helmets. We were warriors racing down the field in full armor. Our teammates cheered while Chariots of Fire played in our heads. We were neck and neck at 40 yards. But at 50 yards, Joel bumped into me, and we bounced off one another like billiard balls. At 80 yards we collided again. Our race ended in a dead tie.

This went on a few times, with Coach Cal moving Joel a little further left with each sprint. But it didn't matter. We still collided downfield and ended in a dead tie.

Finally, Coach Cal put Joel on my right. He blew his whistle. I bolted down the field in a perfectly straight line at Hyde Park, parallel to Linwood Avenue. Out of the corner of my right eye, I could see Joel running at an angle toward the street. Well, he just missed a tree, jumped over some little kids sitting on the sideline, crossed Linwood

Avenue and ran through the front yards of the houses on the other side. We lost sight of him as he cut through some back yards. He ended up somewhere on Michigan Avenue. All of a sudden, he showed up back in the park and we crossed the goal line at the same time!

Coach Cal came up to us both, grinning ear to ear, and privately told us, "Nice job fellas – make sure you both come and see me in the Spring and try out for the track team. Then he winked at me and said, "Simpson – Coach Scaletta coaches the baseball team – you stay away from him!"

I walked home from practice that day with my friend Joel. I asked him why he didn't just run in a straight line. He confided in me that he couldn't, and I don't think he would mind me telling you why. You see, Joel had a medical condition called "strabismus" that prevented him from running in a straight line. For every 100 yards I ran, he ran 110. It didn't bother him at all that we always tied. We all knew that my friend Joel was the fastest cat on the team.

I don't know how many of my teammates knew about Joel's medical condition. Joel knew. I knew. And Coach Cal knew. But nobody ever mentioned it. Nobody ever talked about what Joel couldn't do. We only talked about what he could do. Coach Cal taught us that. He taught us the power of positive thinking. We didn't win a game that year, but we were all winners.

And that's why, when I lay my head on my pillow at night, and I hear Coach Cal blowing that whistle, I forget about the things this middle-aged man with a titanium knee and ceramic hip can't do, and I wake up every morning thinking about all the things I still can do.

Coach Arthur Calandrelli was a great coach and a great man who touched the lives of many young athletes in Niagara Falls. It warms my heart to see his name on the Niagara Falls High School stadium.

Here's to you Coach!

[Whistle blows!]

Faith, Family & Baseball
(A Father, Still and Always)

On Faith

It was just the two of us. My wife was in Florida and his was in heaven. En route to what would be his last Easter dinner in 2009, I noticed that he did the sign of the cross as we drove down Center Street in Lewiston. I figured he was praying that I would take him someplace nice for dinner. On the way home, he did it again, at the same place on the route.

"Why are you doing that dad? Are you thanking God for that great dinner?"

"No son, we just passed the house of the Lord - pay attention!"

I glanced over my shoulder at St. Peter's Roman Catholic Church. My dad did the sign of the cross whenever he passed by any Catholic church, whether he was walking or in a car.

There he was, an old man, a father, still and always, teaching his grown son a lesson.

On Family

He vowed to keep her in sickness and in health. The love of his life suffered from a debilitating illness for the last thirty years of her life. But no worries. He

 worked, he cooked, he cleaned, he nursed, and he loved. And he never complained. You could see the pain in his eyes and the aches in his bones, but still, he never complained. He just did what a loving husband should do. He just did what he had promised to do.

Souvenir du St. Sacrement de Mariage
Leonard Simpson & Blanche Duff
New Bedford, Massachusetts
November 6, 1943

After she passed away, I went to visit him. I noticed that he kept a manilla folder on his kitchen table. Inside were birthday cards for each child and grandchild, carefully selected and purchased well in advance of the special days. He tucked a dollar or two inside of each card and signed them, "Love, Dad" or "Love, Grandpa". I was fifty years old when the birthday card arrived in the mail, on the third anniversary of my mom's passing. Two one-dollar bills fell from the card, tucked inside by a retired factory worker and addressed to his lawyer son. I didn't need the money, but those were the two most meaningful dollars I ever received.

There he was, an old man, a father, still and always, teaching his grown son a lesson.

On Baseball

Late in his life, my brother and I took him to the National Baseball Hall of Fame in Cooperstown. He had never been. As we pushed him in his wheelchair, he regaled us with stories of the greats. I tried to stump him and stopped in front of the most obscure baseball player I could find, some guy from long ago that my brother and I had never heard of.

"Dad, how did this guy ever make it into the Hall?"

"You're right son - he was a pretty good fielder, but he couldn't hit a slider worth a damn!"

My brother and I were stunned and speechless. Amazing!

He came to every one of my Little League games. He bought me my first baseball mitt with S&H green stamps. He played catch with me in the backyard. He cheered me on when we won and consoled me when we lost. He taught me to "win without boasting and lose without excuse".

But my fondest baseball memories will be the many

times I called him while I was watching a Yankees game on TV in my house, and I knew he would be watching in his. We may have been separated by miles, but baseball was a common bond, as long as the Yankees were playing.

If the Yankees hit a home run, he wouldn't even say hello when he picked up the phone.

"Yeah, I saw it!"

If the opposing team hit a home run, he would answer with the same seven words every time ...

"I don't want to talk about it!"

And if the Red Sox hit a home run, he wouldn't even answer the phone!

There he was, my dad, still and always, teaching his son a lesson, about love. He didn't need to answer the phone. He knew I was thinking about him, and he let me know he was thinking about me.

Leonard Paul Simpson was born on February 12, 1921. The Yankees won the pennant that year but lost the World Series. Len wasn't happy.

My dad did the sign of the cross for the last time after saying his evening prayers, just six days after his 89th birthday. A few hours later, on February 19, 2010, he enjoyed his second birthday. He kissed his wife and took her by the hand. Then he shook the hands of Babe Ruth and Lou Gehrig. He had a big smile on his face. The Yankees had won the World Series a few months earlier. His life was complete.

Love you dad, still and always, your son.

What's It Like Dad?

I missed him so much. I just had to know. I just had to ask him. So, when he appeared, I did just that.

"What's it like dad?"

"You mean in heaven?"

"Yes, dad, what's it like in heaven?"

And then he told me … answering all my questions along the way …

"It's a happy place, and very peaceful. No one fights and no one argues. Your mom is here and so are your sisters. Your grandparents are here and so are your aunts and uncles and some of your cousins. A few of your friends are here. Your puppies are here too, Heidi and Lovey and Sheena, and they play all day long. They even play with your cat, Charlie. There is no pain. Pain has been replaced by smiles and laughs and love."

"Are people nice there?"

"Yes, they are, and every one! When St. Peter welcomes you and introduces you to Jesus, Jesus smiles and touches you. When he does this, he forgives you for any unkindness you may have shown during your life on earth. He extracts any bits of meanness, jealousy, greed, and anger from your soul and tosses them to the wind. Over the clouds they fly and then fall away. The only thing you keep is His greatest gift – love!"

"Is everyone playing a harp in heaven, dad?"

"No, they aren't, unless they want to. And if you don't know how to play, one of the angels will touch you, and you will instantly know how to play any instrument you want. And you will play beautifully."

"Is everyone singing in heaven, dad?"

"No, they aren't, unless they want to, and many do want to. And if you don't know how to sing, one of the angels will touch you, and you will instantly know how to sing any song you want, and your voice will be distinctive, and you will sing beautifully."

"Can you walk around in heaven, dad?"

"Yes, you can, if you want to. You can walk on sandy ocean beaches or climb the highest mountains. Or you can run, and never tire. Or you can float. Or you can fly."

"What does everyone look like dad? Do they look the same as when they were here – on their very last day?"

"That's a very good question. You have to understand that when you are on earth your appearance changes as you grow older, but your soul doesn't. When you are in heaven, you get to pick your appearance. You pick any day you want from your days on earth, and you can change it anytime you want to! You can be fifteen on Monday and twenty-five on Tuesday if you want to!"

"Is there baseball in heaven dad?"

"Well, Babe Ruth is here, and Lou Gehrig and Mickey and Ty and Honus and Roberto and Ted and Hank, so what do you think?"

"I think they must have some awesome games!"

"They do son, but there are no teams, it's all pickup games."

"Wow! Who gets picked first?"

"God won't let me tell you that – you'll have to wait and see when you get here!"

The moon was fading, the sun was rising, and he told me he had to go soon, so I had better ask all my important questions.

"Dad, are you with mom?"

"Yes son, love is eternal."

"Can you see me and hear me?"

"I watch over you every day, and so does your mom. We don't see your private moments and we can't see your thoughts and prayers – only God sees those, but we see your joy and sense your pain. We are there when you say our names and even there when you think of us."

"Are you right there in the room?"

"Yes son."

"Even in the bathroom?"

"Don't get smart with me if you want to go to heaven."

"What do I have to do to get there, dad?"

"You have to continue being kind and helping others. Keep smiling and asking people how they are doing. That means more than you know. Love your wife and your daughter, love your friends, and hug them often. Love your puppies too – you know God gave them a special kind of love – the kind you will know when you get here."

"Anything else?"

"Use your gifts, son. God gave them to everyone. Find out which ones he gave to you and then use them to the fullest."

"You mean like my singing voice?"

"No, an angel hasn't touched you yet."

"Dad, when will I see you and mom again?"

The sunlight filtered through my bedroom window.

"Dad?"

"Dad?"

"Dad?"

The drapes fluttered in the morning breeze. They made a soft, comforting sound. I knew he was there.

I opened my eyes to greet the day.

"I love you dad."

Charlie and His Hot Dog

Charlie was only six years old, but his teacher encouraged him to enter his school's Invention Convention. She encouraged all her kids to think of a problem to be solved, and then solve it. She told them to think about the biggest problem in their daily lives and then come up with a solution.

Charlie lived in the inner city. His dad wasn't in the picture. I don't know for sure, but I suspect he never was. His mom did the best she could for Charlie and his older brother Sean. But there wasn't much money to spare – barely enough for groceries and rent. Charlie and Sean depended on the public school for two of their three daily meals. But you don't need money to buy love, and there was plenty of that to go around.

So little Charlie thought long and hard about the problems in his life. Innocence lends perspective. The biggest problem he faced, and solved, surprised his mom, and shocked his teacher.

You see, Charlie loved hot dogs. They were his absolute favorite food. He loved them fresh off the grill, loaded with mustard, ketchup, and relish. He didn't care much for onions or pickles. He was a neat little boy who never left a glass of milk anything but empty, and never left a morsel of food on his plate. It bothered him when he took a bite of his Oscar Mayer dog and ketchup and mustard squirted every which way. It wasn't because his mom yelled at him when it landed on his clean shirt – she didn't - he was just upset that it didn't land in his tummy!

That was a problem for a first grader to solve. And solve it he did. Charlie took a straw and poked it into the middle of a hot dog end to end. He scooped out a straw full of hot dog. He held that dog up to his eye and he could see his mom through the hole in the middle. He cut off an inch of that bored-out hot dog core and set it aside. And then he carefully loaded the inside of that dog with relish. He pushed the relish into the hole and then he squeezed in equal parts ketchup and mustard with an eye dropper. Then he plugged both ends with the bored-out hot dog parts and threw his dog on the grill!

Young Charlie knew he had become an inventor when he took his first bite. Hot dog, mustard, ketchup, and relish flooded his taste buds! He had all four flavors in just one bite – with no mess! Heck, even Reese's Peanut Butter Cups only gave you two flavors in a single bite! His mom smiled with pride as a good mother should. And his big brother told him how smart he was as he took his second bite.

Charlie's mom and brother weren't the only ones impressed by this all-in-one hot dog. Charlie's teacher, Mrs. Baxter, loved it too. And so did the judges - local attorneys, inventors, and businesspeople who volunteered to judge the K-8 Invention Convention that year. There were twenty-nine other inventions on display that day straight from the minds of first graders. But none impressed the judges as much as Charlie's. And how could you not be impressed? Every time a judge stopped by Charlie's display he would take a bite, chew a little, swallow a little and then flash that mustard, ketchup, and relish smile – showing the judges a cross-section of a red, green, and yellow Oscar Mayer hot dog!

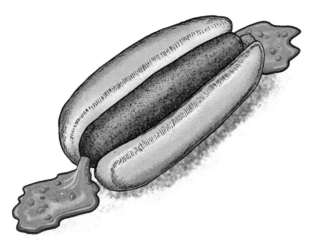

Charlie's all-in-one dog took first place in the first grade at his school, and a few weeks later he wowed the judges again at the city-wide convention at the Buffalo

Museum of Science. Charlie had just finished his twenty-fourth hot dog when the judges awarded him one of the top first grade prizes in the city. That's a lot of hot dogs, and a lot of condiments, for a little guy to swallow.

And then it happened …

The note from the principal told Charlie's mom that he had been selected to represent the City of Buffalo in the statewide Invention Convention. Twenty-five kids from Buffalo would join twenty-five each from Rochester, Syracuse, Albany, and Binghamton at the Strong Museum in Rochester. One hundred and twenty-five of the state's brightest junior inventors would show the world that they could solve problems. They would be treated to a jazz band performance, a magic show, and inspiring stories from successful adult inventors. They would stand at their stations and explain their inventions one-on-one to everyone who stopped by. They would hear the rumor that the famous "snake light" was invented by a fourth grader in Binghamton and demonstrated at one of these conventions, that Black and Decker paid for her patent, and that this young inventor later attended Princeton University, totally paid for by the royalties.

Finally, each young inventor would be called to the stage individually. His or her name would be read aloud, their school and city announced, followed by a few words about the invention as an adult draped a medal around the neck of the beaming child. Parents and grandparents would smile and sometimes cry.

But Charlie's mom had to check the box next to "Will not attend." And then she had to break the news to Charlie. She had no car. She had no way to get Charlie to Rochester. He took it in stride. He was used to disappointment. He didn't shed a tear. He loved his mom. He gave the note to his teacher. But Mrs. Baxter was not the kind of teacher who could sleep easy knowing she sent twenty-four out of twenty-five kids to the big show.

That's when I got the call. The school couldn't provide transportation for liability reasons. But I could.

I'm pretty sure I was the first lawyer Charlie's mom ever met. Our skin colors were different, but that didn't seem to matter to her. She cross-examined me on her front porch for thirty minutes. She asked to see my driver's license. She even took a photo of it. She asked me for a map to show her where we were going. She asked if she could see my cell phone so she could write down my phone number. She took a photo of my license plate and of my minivan. She sized me up and studied me from head to toe. She asked me so many questions that I forgot that I was the lawyer, and she wasn't. I didn't mind. I loved it. She was a mom being a mom.

When the interrogation ended, she knelt down and asked, "Well Charlie, do you want to go to Rochester with

Mr. Bob?" Charlie smiled and said, "Yes mom."

"OK Mr. Bob, you can take Charlie to Rochester under one condition. You have to take Sean too."

I immediately agreed as Sean bolted through the front door, and off we went, the three of us and two-dozen condiment-stuffed hotdogs in a Coleman cooler.

As we drove east on the thruway, Charlie peppered me with questions. He wanted to know all about the inventors I had met and the things they had invented. He wanted to know about college. He asked me if law school was hard and if they gave me a lot of homework.

He paused his questions to stare out the window as we passed by a farm.

"Sean – what are those?"

"Those are cows Charlie."

"Sean – what are those?"

"Those are horses Charlie."

"Sean - what are those?"

"Those are weeping willow trees Charlie."

Cows and horses and weeping willows weren't the only things Charlie experienced for the first time on that Saturday. He honed his public speaking skills. He explained his invention. He listened to a jazz band. He saw a magic show. He heard his name called and he walked onto a stage to receive his inventor's medal as hundreds applauded. I took pictures for his mom. I had asked her to join us, but she had to work.

A few hours later we headed for the parking lot. Sean climbed into the back seat, then Charlie. As I got into the driver's seat Charlie yelled, "Oops!" I turned around just in time to see that Charlie had accidentally sat on six of his stuffed hot dogs, and relish, mustard and ketchup squirted out each end, all over my upholstery. He was petrified. I just smiled and told him, "No worries, Charlie! We can buy you some more hot dogs."

Halfway home and I could tell the kids were hungry. As I pulled into the parking lot, Charlie asked, "Sean – what is that place?"

"That's a restaurant Charlie."

"Have you ever eaten in a restaurant before Charlie?"

"No sir."

They studied the menu silently. They especially studied the prices. They checked their pockets for change. They didn't say a word when the waitress asked them if they had decided.

How could I be so dumb? They thought that they would have to pay. It never occurred to me. I told them they could order anything they wanted. They looked skeptical. I showed them a fifty-dollar bill. Even that didn't satisfy them.

"Mr. Bob, could we each have a hamburger?" (Charlie was tired of hot dogs!)

"Yes Charlie."

"Could we have French fries too?"

"Yes Charlie."

"Could we even have a milk shake?"

"Yes Charlie, and a piece of apple pie for dessert if you like."

Charlie ate his whole hamburger and a large order of fries. Sean did the same. They enjoyed two large chocolate shakes, and then a big piece of apple pie à la mode. There were only six lonely French fries left on Charlie's plate as he took his last bite of pie. And when the waitress came to clear his plate, Charlie asked politely if he could take those six fries home for his mom. "Of course, you can."

Never before had I seen two young boys enjoy a restaurant meal more than these two.

And never before had I enjoyed a restaurant meal as much myself.

Charlie learned an awful lot that day. But I think I may have learned even more.

I think about Charlie every time I take a bite of a hot dog, with mustard, ketchup, and relish. I wonder what he's inventing now.

There's a Car on the Bike Path

It was a beautiful summer day for a bike ride. I was fifteen miles into my usual Sunday 18-mile ride on the Clarence Bike Path and gunning for home. I crossed Main Street heading west and was just about to "thread the needle" between two yellow posts intended to keep cars off the path. To my great surprise, a green car was coming right at me on the path on the other side of the posts. This is different, I thought.

The driver stopped six inches from the posts. My brakes screeched as I stopped my bike about one foot from the driver's front bumper. Behind the wheel was a startled elderly woman, neatly dressed, gray hair, wearing stylish pink glasses peering just above the steering wheel.

I cautiously approached her green Malibu sedan.

"May I help you?" I asked.

"Yes," she said, "I think I'm lost. Could you please move those yellow posts so I can get through?"

"I'm sorry, Miss, but I don't think I can move them. They are made of steel and embedded in concrete. I think you have to back up."

"Oh, I don't think I could manage that," she said.

I empathized. Her car was wedged between two chain-linked fences, with only about twelve inches of clearance on either side. It was unclear how far she would have to drive in reverse before she could turn her car around.

By now a crowd was gathering. It's not every day you see a car wedged on a bike path. I looked around for Richard Petty, but he was nowhere to be found. I introduced myself to the driver who told me her name was Deloris. She told me she was on her way to a baby shower and must have made a wrong turn. I thought to myself, there must be fifty ways to get to that baby shower, Deloris, but this surely wasn't one of them.

I offered to back her car up if she would walk my bike. But when she got out of her car and hobbled up to my bike with her walker I reconsidered.

A bystander jumped in and offered to walk my bike.

I had to walk sideways between Deloris' car and the fence. I exhaled and squished myself into the driver's seat and Deloris did the same on the passenger side.

There were about thirty people in front of the car by now. Some were munching on popcorn. Others were taking photographs with their phones. I rolled down the window and asked, "Would you all like to squeeze by before I move the car?"

But there were no takers. They all seemed intent on

enjoying the Sunday afternoon entertainment. Some of them were placing bets on the whole operation.

I instructed Deloris to buckle her seatbelt and I did the same. I placed the car in reverse and slowly started to roll. It is never really clear in a situation like this if the rear-view mirror or the side view mirror is the most helpful. Of course, I had never been in a situation quite like this before. I couldn't decide so I just stuck my head out the driver's side window and looked rearward. I figured that we would be OK if I could keep her car parallel to the fence on my side of the car.

It took us a very long time to drive the Malibu backwards at one mile an hour for fifty yards. We made small talk during the voyage. Deloris told me about the gifts she bought for the baby shower. We talked about her kids and grandkids. She was very personable for a person stuck in a car with a stranger on a bike path. At first, she was a little embarrassed but seemed better when I reassured her that I rode my bike on this path every Sunday and that I had seen this sort of thing before. At one point I made the mistake of glancing through the front windshield. The crowd had grown to about 100, including a television news crew, and three Sheriff's deputies on horseback, and they were all walking slowly toward the car. It looked like a scene from *The Walking Dead*, except with live people. I never looked forward again.

At the 50-yard mark the path widened a bit. A few bystanders guided me in a nerve-wracking 10-point turn. It took about ten minutes to turn the car 180 degrees. Now we just had to get the car over the pedestrian bridge with six inches of clearance on each side of the car. The bridge carried the path fifty feet above the road below. I couldn't help but wonder how Deloris got the car over the bridge in the first place, but I thought it an inopportune time to inquire. I privately wondered if the bridge would support us as we crossed. I didn't want to worry her, but I feared we might drop suddenly onto a passing car below.

And then it happened ...

We finally got to the other side of the bridge and the path widened. The crowd applauded and Deloris gave me a big kiss on the cheek as I gave her the keys and said good-bye. She thanked me for my service as I mounted my bicycle and headed for home.

By the way, I always ride on bike paths to avoid cars.

Telephone Calls
(Car Insurance Salesman)

While hard at work in my office yesterday afternoon – writing a patent application for one of my favorite clients, with drawings displayed on my second monitor, and the patent application displayed on my laptop which was – on my lap – my cell phone rang. Caller ID showed a Niagara Falls number. I ALWAYS answer calls from Niagara Falls phone numbers. I'm hoping it is a call from DiCamillo's, Sammy's, Viola's or Fortuna's telling me I've won a free loaf of bread, pizza, steak and cheese sub or spaghetti dinner.

"Hello!"

"Hello sir, this is John calling from 'We sell auto insurance for less!' How are you today?"

"Great John! Thank you for asking. I'm working on a utility patent application for a client of mine. I've written a broad independent claim to the invention and ten dependent claims. I thought about writing a Jepson claim, and I toyed with writing a Markush claim but decided against it. I've finished the claims, the drawings, the abstract and am just about to start writing the detailed description of the invention."

"That's interesting. What is the invention?"

"I could tell you John, but then I would have to kill you and bury your body and hope no one investigates because if you take notes about the invention and the police find those notes in your pocket when they find your body, I will probably be disbarred for disclosing confidential client information and then for murdering you to cover up the breach."

"I understand. I am wondering if you would be interested in saving money on your auto insurance? If you answer a few questions about your current policy, I have a network of insurers and a sophisticated computer program that will find you the lowest rates."

"Gee John, I don't think that would work for me."

"Why not?"

"Because I always buy the most expensive auto-insurance policy I can find."

"Well, sir, I am sure that I can save you money."

"In fact, John, I always buy the most expensive item in the store when I shop. I just bought a Wolf Gourmet Countertop Toaster Oven from Williams-Sonoma for $679.95 because it was the most expensive toaster oven I could find from a store that could arrange delivery when my wife wasn't at home. I also always buy the most expensive men's underwear made of Supima Cotton from Brooks Brothers."

"I'm sure I can probably save you a couple of hundred dollars a year on your auto insurance, with very low deductibles."

"My life philosophy, John, is that a consumer should always overpay for everything he buys. I believe that there is a direct correlation between price and quality. That's why I buy only hand-made shoes from Allen-Edmonds in Wisconsin. Sure, they cost a few hundred dollars a pair but after five years you can have them recrafted for $100. They come back looking brand new and then you get another five years out of them, and they never go out of style."

"We are talking about a few hundred dollars a year in savings!"

"John, do you ever shop on Amazon?"

"Why, yes sir, I do."

"Have you ever noticed the filter at the top right of the page where you can sort by price – lowest to highest or highest to lowest?"

"Yes – I use that all the time."

"How do you sort John?"

"From lowest price to highest price."

"John, did you happen to run out of toilet paper

during the early days of the pandemic?"

"Why yes I did."

"It's because of your Amazon filter John. I ALWAYS sort from high price to low price. You would not believe how many expensive rolls of toilet paper I was able to buy when the shelves were bare at the local grocery stores. Some of the rolls I bought were even monogrammed. I never ran out."

"I'm never going to sell you an auto insurance policy - am I?"

"No John, I'm afraid not. But if there is ever a run on toilet paper again you might want to keep my phone number on hand. I'll help you out!

Telephone Calls
(Real Estate Broker)
(Love Means Never Having to Say You're Sorry)

(Cell phone rings)

"Hello!"

"Hello, is this Mr. Simpson?"

"Yes, it is."

"Hello sir, this is Marco Martinez Guerrero calling you from North Palm Beach. How are you today?"

"I am fine and dandy, and how are you doing on this beautiful Friday, Marco?"

"I'm fine sir."

"May I call you Marco?"

"Yes, you may sir."

"Great! And you can call me Bob if you like."

"OK, thank you. Mr. Simpson, I am wondering if you are the owner of a condo at 132 Lakeshore Drive?"

"Yes, I am. It is a beautiful place."

"Yes sir, I know it is."

"I can see Jack Nicklaus' house from my balcony."

"Really sir?"

"Yes, and I can see Tiger Woods' yacht down in the harbor!"

"You can? Is it a nice boat?"

"Yes, it is. But it is only half as big as his last boat."

"It is?"

"Yes, it is Marco."

"I wonder why he bought a smaller boat?"

"He cheated on his wife, Marco. When you cheat on your wife, you deserve a smaller boat, don't you think?"

"Yes, I guess you're right."

"Mr. Simpson, I am wondering if you have ever thought about selling your condo at 132 Lakeshore Drive?"

"Yes Marco – I think about it every day!"

"Wow! Why is that sir?"

"Because I live next door to my mother-in-law."

"Oh, I'm sorry sir."

"Me too."

"So, you really would consider selling your condo sir?"

"In a heartbeat!"

"May I ask what your selling price would be?"

"You may ask but I am not allowed to tell you."

"Pardon me? Why are you not allowed to tell me?"

"Because I married a Certified Public Accountant."

"I don't understand?"

"Are you married Marco?"

"No sir, I am not."

"I'm sorry Marco. You know, being married means you have a fifty per cent chance of getting a date on Saturday night!"

"OK, I'll keep that in mind. But why can't you tell me how much you want for your condo?"

"Marco, when you marry an accountant, it puts you on a very special path in life. You forget what everything costs. You don't pay your bills yourself anymore. You don't keep a checkbook. You just sign a tax form your wife gives you every April 15. You don't even get a paycheck."

"Oh, I am so sorry sir."

"It's OK Marco. I get an allowance. I get $100 a week whether I need it or not."

"I'm sorry sir."

"Marco, you say 'I'm sorry' a lot."

"I'm sorry sir."

"Marco, are you dating anyone?"

"Yes sir, I am dating a beautiful woman named Laurianne."

"That's lovely, Marco. Are you in love?"

"I think I am sir."

"That's beautiful! You know, Marco, love means never having to say you're sorry."

"What?"

"Ali MacGraw and Ryan O'Neal. You should Google it."

"OK."

"Sir, would you sell me your condo?"

"I'm sorry Marco, but you would have to ask my wife about that. She co-owns the condo with me, and she handles all real estate transactions for our family."

"OK sir, can you give me her phone number?"

[At this point, my wife, sitting in the adjoining office, jumps to her feet, glares at me through the glass door, and starts impersonating an NFL back judge indicating an incomplete pass.]

"I'm sorry, Marco, but my wife is frantically signaling that I am not allowed to give you her phone number. She has written the word "garage" on a piece of paper and is holding it up to the glass between us."

"I don't understand sir."

"Marco, when you are married and about to do something really stupid and your wife writes the word "garage" on a big piece of paper or even on a Post-it note, that is an indication as to where you will be sleeping tonight."

"I am sorry sir."

"You're sorry?? I live in Buffalo!"

"I don't understand."

"It's snowing here Marco. It starts snowing here the end of August and continues snowing until mid-June. Even my dogs wouldn't sleep in the garage tonight."

"Oh!"

(Whispering)

"Marco – how much can I pay you to buy my mother-in-law's condo next door to mine?"

"I don't know sir."

"I'm sorry."

"Me too."

Telephone Calls
(AMEX Representative)

We were sitting in our car outside the Olympic Restaurant, when my wife reminded me, "You've got to call AMEX!"

"Now?"

"Now would be good."

"But I'm hungry!"

"It will only take a few minutes."

"But I don't know the phone number."

"It's on the back of your card."

"Oh."

Beep-beep-beep---beep-beep-beep----beep-beep-beep-beep.

"Please enter your account number for better service."

"I don't know my account number."

"Hand me the phone."

Beep-beep-beep-beep----beep-beep-beep-beep-beep-beep---beep-beep-beep-beep-beep."

"How do you know the account number?"

"I'm holding the statement in my hand."

"Oh."

"Hello, this is Delores from American Express. Please know that this call may be recorded for quality control purposes. How may I help you today?"

"Hello Delores. My name is Bob. I don't really know how you may help me today. My wife made me call you. Would you like to speak with her?"

"I'm sorry Bob, but your wife isn't an authorized user on your account, so I can't speak with her unless you authorize her."

"Ok, I hereby authorize you, Delores, of American Express, to speak with my wife, Ellen. Do you need that in writing?"

"No, I don't. But I'm afraid it's not that simple Bob. First, I have to verify your identity. What is your full name?"

"My full name is Robert Paul Simpson. My confirmation name is Peter. My friends call me Bob. Almost no one ever calls me Robert except my mother who always called me 'Robert Paul' whenever I did something wrong, and a friend of mine named Shawn in Huntsville, Alabama, because I am his lawyer and I think he thinks he gets better legal advice from a 'Robert' than from a 'Bob', so I go along with it."

"I see. Thank you for that Mr. Simpson. Can you please give me the last four digits of your Social Security number? Sure, it's beep-beep-beep-beep. Do you need the last four numbers of my wife's Social Security number? Because I memorized those thirty-seven years ago and I am quite proud that I still remember them."

"No Bob, that won't be necessary. Now, can you please tell me your mother's middle name?"

"Sure, it's Stella. Can you please speak to my wife now?"

"Not yet. What was your mother's maiden name?"

"My mother's maiden name was Duff. But she was not related to Duff's chicken wings on Sheridan Drive. It's too bad because we really like Duff's wings, but we still have to pay full price. I am sorry, Delores, but all this talk about my mom is getting me kind of teary eyed. Can you please speak to my wife now? I think I'm going to cry."

"Not quite yet. I need to know your birthday – month, day, and year."

"March 29, 1956. You know, Delores, my mom passed away on my birthday a few years ago."

"Oh Mr. Simpson, I am so sorry to hear that."

"It's OK. At first, I wondered why she couldn't wait one more day, but then I realized it really wasn't up to her. I've made peace with it. It's kind of an honor. Is that too much information for you Delores? I hope you don't think that I'm fixated on my mother or anything. It's just that every question you are asking me seems to relate to my mother. I'm sorry. I am out and out crying now, Delores. Can you please speak to my wife?"

"No, not yet, but it's OK. I lost my mom too.

I understand."

"Now before I talk to your wife, can you please read me the three digits from the back of your card?"

"I'm sorry Delores but I can't do that."

"Why not?"

"I don't have the card."

"Was it lost or stolen?"

"No Delores, the card is somewhere at home, but my wife won't tell me where it is because she doesn't want me to use it."

"I see. Are you OK with that?"

"Delores, I forgot to tell you that you are on speaker phone and my wife is sitting right next to me. She is listening to our whole conversation to make sure I don't say something stupid. Of course, I'm OK with it. She is a Certified Public Accountant and I am not. We got married in 1984 and she handles all the financial stuff for our family."

"Oh, that's nice. That sounds like a nice arrangement."

"She does a good job, but you know I haven't seen a paycheck in 37 years!"

"Oh, I'm sorry Bob."

"It's OK Delores. She gives me $100 a week whether I need it or not and lets me keep anything I get from taking pop bottles back to the store."

"That's nice Bob. What is pop?"

"Delores, where are you located?"

"I'm in Boston Bob, why?"

"Are you a Patriots fan?"

"Why yes, I am, and you?"

"I'm in Buffalo, Delores, with all that that entails, and 'pop' is what you would call 'soda'. It's OK that you like the Patriots, Delores. My mom was from New Bedford, and my daughter went to college in Boston and my brother-in-law lived in Cambridge for many years."

"Oh. that's a relief. For a minute there I thought you weren't going to speak with me anymore because you were a Buffalo Bills fan."

"We are die-hard Bills fans Delores – season ticket holders since the sixties. But you seem very nice, and I am very much enjoying our conversation. But I am getting hungry. Can you speak with my wife now please?"

"Not yet Bob. First, I have to tell you that now that your wife is an authorized user on your American Express Card, and even though she can charge whatever she wants to your card, you are personally responsible for all the charges on this account. She doesn't have to pay the bill. You do! If you don't pay the bill, you will be in big trouble. Do you understand these rights and responsibilities as I have explained them to you?"

"Yes – it sort of sounds a lot like the Miranda rights I heard on Adam-12 yesterday."

"What's Adam-12?"

"It's a police TV show from the 70s."

"Oh, I didn't know that Bob – I was born in 1984. Now that you understand your responsibilities and that you can be sued, arrested, and sent to jail if you run up your credit card bill buying stamps for your collection, Brooks Brothers shirts or chess sets that you don't need, is there any other family member or employee you would like me to authorize and send a credit card too?"

"Lord no Delores! How do you know all this stuff about me? Please talk to my wife now!"

"Sure Bob. Hello Mrs. Simpson, how may I help you?"

"Could you please link this account to our other AMEX accounts?"

"Let's see. I'm afraid I'll need your husband's permission to do this."

(Ellen whispering) "Robert P. Simpson, you give Delores permission to link these accounts right now!"

"Hi Delores, what color is the card on this account that you are linking?"

"It's green Bob, why."

"I don't think I've ever seen the green card. I've seen my wife's gold card. And I have a platinum card. It's not that I like to show off or anything, I just like metal cards better than plastic. I don't really know why. I also prefer leather to vinyl, and wood chess pieces to plastic. Do you think that's pretentious Delores?"

"Not at all Bob. May I link your green card account to your gold and platinum accounts?"

"Sure."

"Maybe I should speak with your wife again."

"Thank God!"

"Mrs. Simpson, I've linked your cards. You are all set."

"Thank you, Delores. Do you need to speak with my husband again?"

"No that's alright. We have it all recorded, and he has been on speaker phone here for the past thirty minutes. My colleagues are rolling on the floor. You two just made our day!"

"Aww that's sweet Delores. Thank you!"

"You are welcome. Good-bye."

"Good-bye."

(Thirty minutes after pulling into the Olympic Restaurant parking lot) …

"May I take your order?"

"Yes, my wife will have a turkey sandwich with a fruit cup on the side and I'll have a Western sandwich on white toast with French fries and brown gravy on the side."

"Anything else?"

"Are you a Bills fan?"

"Of course!"

"Do you need to know my birthday?"

"Not really."

"We're good then."

Telephone Calls
(Caribbean Cruise and the Convict)

2:21 P.M. 3/8/2021 Caller ID Frewsburg, NY

[Prerecorded female voice]: "Hello – you qualify for a free Caribbean Cruise to an exotic destination of your choice. Press "0" to speak to an operator."

"0"

"Hello sir, this is Jason, how are you today?"

"I am fine Jason. I just enjoyed doing fifty push-ups and a game of solitaire in my room. Later I'm going to research the law on Miranda rights."

"That's nice sir – I am calling today to offer you a free two-week Caribbean Cruise to an exotic destination of your choice. We can take you to Cancun, Bermuda, the Virgin Islands, the Bahamas or Miami, Florida. How does that sound to you, sir?"

"That sounds wonderful Jason. Can you also arrange for a Presidential Pardon?"

"Yes, sir, I can!"

"That's great, because I am currently serving two concurrent life sentences for murder in a federal

penitentiary."

"Oh, I'm sorry sir, who did you murder?"

"I murdered the Captain of a Caribbean Cruise ship for taking me to Iceland in January and then I sank his boat. I also murdered the telemarketer who sold me the cruise."

"Oh, I'm sorry sir, but we can take you to a tropical island where you can enjoy a sunny, sandy beach!"

"That sounds really nice – I haven't been allowed outside my cell since the jury verdict."

"Well, sir, you don't have to use these free tickets right away."

"Oh, that's good, I am eligible for parole in 2056."

[Dial tone sound]

"Hello?"

"Hello?"

"Hello?"

The Earthquake and the Toothbrush

I had just settled into my early evening routine. I nestled into my black leather recliner in my man cave in front of my Samsung 65" ultra high-definition flat screen at precisely 6:58 p.m. on Wednesday evening. I clicked my remote to tune in Channel 37, the Andy Griffith Show, and clicked again to learn that I was about to enjoy the episode where Barney Fife buys a motorcycle from an army surplus store so he can catch speeders on the highway outside of Mayberry.

I am such a creature of habit. I've seen this episode a hundred times. I know every line by heart. I know that Barney keeps his bullet in his front shirt pocket. I know that the citizens of Mayberry are going to make fun of him when he shows up at the courthouse with his goggles, helmet, motorcycle boots, and elbow-length leather gloves. But I will laugh out loud at Barney just as I have a hundred times before. I love this show. I love Andy, Barney, Opie, Aunt Bee, and Floyd. I love Thelma

Lou and Helen too. I'm still hoping that Barney will marry Thelma Lou and Andy will marry Helen and live happily ever after. It so reminds me of my childhood and the small town feel that I remember and still yearn for.

Barney had just brought Andy outside the courthouse door to show him the Sheriff Department's new "motorsicle." The townsfolk were making fun of Barney, his costume, and his vehicle.

And then it happened …

My man cave started to shake and rumble. The floor shook beneath my feet. Missy and Mia sensed the danger and jumped to their paws. Their instincts kicked in as they ran circles around me, herding and protecting me like their ancestors protected their flocks of sheep. It was a low rumble, an annoying vibration. It was probably only a 4.2 on the Richter scale, and then it stopped as suddenly as it appeared.

My puppies returned to their beds. The excitement subsided. Barney went out on patrol. Andy returned to his desk to figure out a way to get rid of that motorcycle.

I took one bite of a still warm Toll House chocolate chip cookie that I had just made with my new Wolf Gourmet Toaster Oven.

And then it happened …

The aftershock! I had heard from my friend in Alaska, Laura Mendola, that this could happen. She reports regularly on these scary earthquakes, and I know I am among many of her friends and former classmates who pray for her and her family. I had never before experienced an earthquake myself, or an aftershock, but I was sure this was my first.

The dogs started herding me again as the wall adjacent my chair started to vibrate. Curiosity got the better of me and I decided to search for the epicenter. On the other side of the wall is my own personal man cave shower stall. It's made of fiberglass and aluminum. It is a stall that only a former high school varsity football player can appreciate. And boy was it vibrating! It was clearly directly atop the epicenter of an 8.2 Richter scale major earthquake in Amherst, New York. I was sure it would take down the rafters as resonance set in, and then the whole upstairs, mother-in-law and all, would collapse on me and my beloved Shelties.

And then it stopped.

And then it started again.

And then it stopped.

And then it started again.

It was then that I did what any classically trained and college educated engineer would do. I called our contractor, Dan Hooper, and asked for advice. Dan could build and fix anything and everything. If anyone on the planet could fix an earthquake in my man cave, it was Dan. And he was quick with advice.

"Unplug your primary sump pump! Then unplug your secondary sump pump! I'll be over in the morning to check them out!" Dan was so smart! Of course, it wasn't an earthquake. It was the sump pump. How embarrassing.

And then it happened, again …

The vibration was so loud this time that it drowned out the whistling theme song of the next Andy Griffith Show episode. It wasn't the sump pump! The wall was vibrating again! Could it be? Oh no – not my right-channel wall-mounted Klipsch surround sound speaker. My engineering education and experience kicked in. I switched the sound from my eight Klipsch speakers to my anemic television speaker. But the sound continued, and so did my frantic text messages to my contractor. By now Ellen had joined me in the cave. She has a knack for showing up during these emergencies to calm me down.

I imbibed a shot of my prized Dalmore Cigar Malt Scotch Whiskey, summoned my courage and entered the shower stall fully dressed. I was sure I would fall through a sinkhole and never see my family again. I paused and looked around. The whole fiberglass enclosure was vibrating. It was very, very scary.

And there it was …

Sitting in the cup-holder on the stall wall next to the toothpaste …

It was my Philips Sonicare DiamondClean rechargeable ultrasonic toothbrush, White Edition, Model HX9332. It had turned itself on! It had put itself into self-cleaning mode. My razor and toothpaste tubes were dancing to the rhythm. I reached over and turned it off. I contemplated never coming out of the shower stall. My wife was sitting on the couch, anxiously awaiting my return. She was clearly concerned about my safety. I contemplated fifty different lies to tell her. But, with the exception of the true cost of my eBike from Germany, I have never lied to my wife in thirty-six years of marriage.

So, I swallowed my pride, took out my phone, and took a photograph of my vibrating ultrasonic toothbrush. I sent it in a text message to my contractor. His wife is still laughing. So is mine.

Because The Gun Went Off Accidentally

I first met Steve Vandervelden in the first few days of law school. Like me, Steve always sat in the back row of every class – no doubt preparing for an early exit from tort or contract law if necessary. He wore a bandana around his head to every class. He looked like a throwback to the 60s. Quite frankly I was worried about him. It's not that he wore the same bandana every day. He didn't. He wore a different bandana, a different color and pattern depending on his mood. It was quite a fashion statement, and it worked. Professors were afraid to call on him. I hung out in his shadow, hoping they wouldn't call on me either.

I worried about Steve for the first two years of law school. It wasn't the bandana that worried me. It was the fact that, even though I sat right next to him in every class, and we were partners in the brightest study group ever to walk the corridors of O'Brian Hall, I never, ever, saw Steve crack open a book. He just sat there in every class, eyes wide open, with an infectious smile, listening and watching, taking it all in, and memorizing it all. Once in a while he would scribble a few notes on a notepad, but he only did that to appease and comfort me.

We did everything together. We sat right next to each other in every class: criminal law, constitutional law, civil procedure, and real property. We taught each other federal tax law. To this day, Steve is an expert on the deductibility of travel expenses. We were Moot Court partners together. He passed every class – most with flying colors. I don't know how he did it. Because, as I mentioned, I never saw him open a book.

It was in our third and final year that I learned that I need not worry. Steve was my partner in our trial technique class. This was a special course offered by the school in a mock courtroom. It was taught by experienced trial lawyers. It was where we all learned how to argue in a courtroom, how to examine and cross-examine witnesses, and how to persuade a jury of our client's cause. It was where all future litigators cut their teeth and learned their trade. And, for some students, like me, it is where we decided that we really didn't want a life of arguing in courtrooms.

Our course culminated in a mock trial in a real-life, New York State Supreme Court courtroom in downtown Buffalo. The trial was presided over by a real Supreme Court judge, and heard by a jury of twelve high school students – all girls. Our client was a jealous husband, accused of murdering his wife who he believed was cheating on him with the milkman. The clues were surely there – way too much chocolate milk, cottage cheese and half-and-half showing up in their refrigerator week after week.

We had a weak case. The facts did not favor us. Our only flimsy defense was that the gun discharged accidentally.

I handled the opening statement; Steve had the closing. I handled direct-examination, and Steve had the cross-examination. And Steve handled all the objections. Steve was a master of objections. He had memorized Wigmore's Treatise on Evidence and he knew all the objections. He objected all the time. "Irrelevant!", "Without foundation!", "That's a stupid question and he shouldn't have to answer!" Steve knew them all.

Steve had an interesting way of objecting. He sat in his chair, on the edge of his seat, carefully listening to every question the prosecutor asked. As soon as he heard something objectionable, he rose from his seat. He bounced up and down as he decided whether to object. Once he decided, he jumped to his feet just as the prosecutor uttered his last word. He bellowed, "Objection, your Honor" before the witness had a chance to answer. Frankly, Steve bounced up and down so much during the trial that our table vibrated across the floor of the courtroom and ended up just a few feet away from the twelve high school girls in the jury box. They didn't seem to mind. They were enjoying Steve's objections as much as the rest of us.

It all came down to the closing argument. Our client was facing twenty-five years to life. He was sweating bullets. He closed his eyes and said a prayer as Steve rose to address the jury. Steve had memorized his closing statement and rehearsed it a dozen times before the trial. The jury of twelve high school seniors were hanging on his every word. Steve read their faces and looked into their eyes. Frankly, even I could see that every one of them would have married Steve if he would only ask. A few of them giggled as he gazed their way.

And then it happened ...

Steve went off script. He totally shot from the hip. He had them and he knew it! So, Steve uttered the most reasonable, rational, logical argument ever heard in New York State Supreme Court up to that time.

"Ladies of the jury. I can see how smart you are. And I can see that you have been paying attention. So, I am going to ask you just one simple question that I know you all know the answer to."

"Do you know why the gun went off accidentally?"

[Steve paused for effect as twelve high school girls in the jury box waited for his answer with bated breath.]

"Because the gun went off accidentally!"

Yep! All twelve jurors nodded affirmatively in unison. I couldn't believe it! The defendant looked to the heavens and did a quick sign of the cross.

Steve had basically just argued that our client was not guilty… because our client was not guilty! And, after five minutes of deliberation, the judge asked the jury forewoman, "Lady forewoman, has the jury reached a verdict?"

"Yes, your honor, we have. We, the jury, find the defendant not guilty, and we also think that Steven is very cute and awesome!"

I couldn't agree more. Steve is awesome. And, after a thirty-four-year career as an Assistant District Attorney in Westchester County where he served our state and that county with distinction, he is now brightening our days with beautiful photographs of ballet dancers. His work is breathtaking. My wife tells me he is still cute too.

Heads We Go To Class/ Tails We Go To Breakfast!

Professor Mugel was really old! He was almost ancient! He was sixty-two years old in 1986 when we entered our third year of law school! He had been teaching for a very long time when my friends and I decided to take his course on "Future Interests". We figured that someone who was that old and had been teaching for that long had to be good.

This was not a decision we entered into lightly. Future Interests is generally regarded by most law students as the single most dull and boring law school course that a student can take. Even tax law doesn't compare. Second-year students have been known to fall asleep and fall off their chairs during this class. Some third-year students have fallen asleep and missed graduation altogether.

Future Interests is a specialized species of real property law. You study life estates, fee simples, remainders, and reversions. You learn all about the beguiling Rule Against Perpetuities, which all law students fear because we know we will be asked about it on the bar exam and absolutely no one in my graduating class of 285 students had any clue what a Perpetuity was, let alone understood the Rule Against it. But, if anybody did, it was Professor Mugel, so we signed up.

This particular class met every Friday and Saturday morning at 8:00 a.m. in Room 106 in O'Brian Hall. No college or law student enjoys 8 a.m. classes. But we showed up ten minutes early for the first class and were greeted at the door by the Professor himself.

He wore a dashing navy-blue-three-piece suit, a starched white shirt and thin blue tie hanging down perfectly straight from a symmetrical full Windsor knot. I suspect he had an old gold pocket watch tucked away in his vest pocket, but I never saw it. His black shoes were perfectly shined, and he wore very stylish glasses. He reminded us of Professor Kingsfield from The Paper Chase, except nicer. We knew we were in the presence of a lawyer's lawyer. He was a legend, after all, one of the founding partners of his own prominent firm.

To our great surprise, we made it through the first class totally awake. My study group buddies, Steve and Mike, only yawned twice. Me too. This was a fascinatingly boring class. But Professor Mugel tried his best to explain it all to us. He loved this stuff, and he wanted us to love it too. And he gave us our tuition's worth. He lectured us and told us fifty-year-old war stories for exactly ninety minutes. Then he tucked his textbook and lecture notes into a battle-worn leather briefcase. I suspect his parents may have given him that briefcase when he graduated from law school decades before I was even born.

After that first class we decided to celebrate over breakfast and review what we had learned. We went to the old Country Café on Niagara Falls Boulevard. It was a dive of a place, but you could get a great ham and cheese omelet or biscuits and gravy for five bucks.

Steve asked the question over coffee:

"Do you think the old professor wears a three-piece suit every day?"

Mike and I were sure that he did. Steve wasn't so sure.

"Even on Saturday?" "No way!"

"Five dollars says he does!"

And so, it began. We now had a reason to go to class on Saturday morning. And we did. And he did. The professor wore a beautiful gray pinstriped suit on that sunny and warm September Saturday morning. Steve lost five dollars that day, but Mike and I treated him to breakfast.

Try as we might, and teach as he did, we just couldn't bring ourselves to make it through every class awake. It wasn't the professor – it was the material. It was so damn boring that it should have never been made into laws in the first place. We talked about leaving law school altogether. Mike was going to charter a fishing boat in the Thousand

Islands; Steve was going to be a famous photographer of dancers in New York City; and I was going to become a writer of short stories in Cheektowaga. But our wives and girlfriends intervened, and made us go to class.

So, of course, we went to every Friday morning class – all twelve of them. On the fourth Friday of the semester, on the biggest and most important day in our beloved Future Interests class, the professor announced, "Today I am going to teach you all about the Rule Against Perpetuities!" We waited with bated breath as he began his lecture.

He patiently explained that the elements of the rule originated in England in the seventeenth century but that the rule didn't really crystallize into a single rule until the nineteenth century. We were on the edges of our seats by then. "Tell us!" "Tell us!" We all chanted in harmony.

And then he did:

"No interest is good unless it must vest, if at all, not later than twenty-one years after some life in being at the creation of the interest."

"Huh?" "What?" "That's it?"

Never before in our law school careers were our bubbles of curiosity punctured with such a sharp pin. We looked to our classmates for an explanation, but none was to be had. No one, not a *cum laude, magna cum laude* or *summa cum laude* wannabe had any idea what the professor was talking about. The members of the Law Review tried to act like they knew, but they didn't have a clue. No law school student in the history of American jurisprudence, with the possible exception of Oliver Wendell Holmes, ever understood it on the first try.

It was time for breakfast. It was time to consider alternative careers.

But our wives and girlfriends wouldn't let us quit, so we promised that we wouldn't. We devised a plan instead.

At precisely 7:30 a.m. every Saturday morning for the remainder of the semester, a fisherman, a photographer, and a storyteller met outside the rear entrance of O'Brian Hall. Steve brought the quarter. Mike made the call. I picked the restaurant. Steve flipped the quarter two feet into the air. We watched with excitement as it bounced off the ground.

Heads we went to class – tails we went to breakfast!

We missed a whole lot of Saturday morning classes that semester, but we enjoyed a whole bunch of pancakes, eggs, toast, and coffee. We tried to figure out the Rule Against Perpetuities by ourselves, but usually ended up talking about our Buffalo Bills or Steve's New York Giants. We wondered if we went to enough classes to pass the exam. It wasn't like me to miss so many classes. It wasn't like me not to do the assigned reading. But Steve assured me that we could learn it on our own.

I trusted Steve. He knew how to cram for a test. And

so we met on the eve of our final examination in Future Interests. Steve's textbook was a virgin white. It had never been opened. I, myself, had only done forty percent of the assigned reading. Steve, Mike, and I had only attended fourteen of the twenty-four classes. These were desperate times.

We pulled an all-nighter in the School of Business building. Steve told me it was the only way. We taught ourselves Future Interests on a chalkboard for twelve straight hours. We memorized the whole damn book. We headed home at 4 a.m. and grabbed a few hours' sleep before our 8 a.m. final exam.

And then it happened …

Professor Mugel met us at the classroom door. Mike had already taken his seat.

"Where are your textbooks fellas?"

Steve looked at me and I looked at him. We had no idea this was an open book exam! We had skipped that class. If we had known, we would not have spent all those hours memorizing everything in the book! Steve didn't miss a beat. "Our textbooks sort of fell apart from all the studying we did this semester!"

The professor smiled at us. "No worries – you can borrow my copy and share it."

I received an honors grade in Future Interests. Steve and Mike did too. We all studied for the bar exam together.

Mike became a public defender and a fisherman. Steve became an assistant district attorney and an acclaimed photographer of dancers. I wrote a few patents and told a few stories.

I'm sixty-four years old now. I teach a course at O'Brian Hall at the law school. I am old, almost ancient in the eyes of my young students. I bring coffee and donuts to my morning classes for them, just in case! I still have no idea what the Rule Against Perpetuities is all about.

P.S. Seven years out of law school I had the honor of practicing law in Professor Mugel's firm. He had slowed down a bit, but he still wore a suit to work every day. I would stop in and visit with him once a week. I confessed what I had done on some of those Saturday mornings and apologized. He laughed. He told me he knew, and he wished he could have joined us for breakfast. Years after I left his firm to start my own, I would now and then receive a phone call from a new client – referred by Professor Mugel. He continued teaching until he died at age eighty-five. He was a lawyer's lawyer.

Mike Farrell, Steve Vandervelden, Robert Simpson (l,r)

University at Buffalo School of Law

Graduation Day – May 17, 1987

The Super Glued Attorney

It seemed like such a good idea. It seemed like such an easy fix. The desk had a loose vinyl strip along its front edge just begging to be glued. I wanted to fix it for our new tenant. I wanted to make my wife proud.

I carefully squeezed the Super Glue into the tiny space between the strip and the edge of the desk. One inch, two inches, three inches and more, slowly spreading the glue with a paper clip. And then the squeeze, first with my fingers and then with my toes, holding the strip in place until the glue set. "One Mississippi, two Mississippi, three Mississippi ..." Around "four Mississippi" it occurred to me that I had no idea how many Mississippi's it would take for the glue to set. I hadn't read the instructions on the package of glue. In fact, I've never met a guy who has ever read the instructions. At "eight Mississippi" I started to get tired. At "twenty-seven Mississippi" I sort of nodded off. At "thirty-eight Mississippi" I woke up and stepped back to admire my work.

And then it happened ...

I noticed some adhesive labels stuck on the top of the desk. There were four of them near the rear edge. No worries. I was prepared. I had brought a brand-new bottle of Goo Gone to the job site. I brought a utility scraper knife too. I even had a circular-saw, but it turned out I didn't need it. I reached over to the stuck labels and went to work. It is good to saturate an adhesive label with Goo Gone. It helps to shout encouragement too.

I soaked and scraped those labels for a good twenty minutes. Soak and scrape and wipe and then soak and scrape and wipe some more. It takes real elbow grease to remove adhesive labels from the top of a desk. It takes time too. Time enough to wonder why someone stuck them there in the first place. They had no useful function that I could discern.

At last, the labels were gone. So was the Goo.

And then it happened, again ...

I tried to get up from my chair. But I couldn't move. I looked down to find my shirt completely Super Glued to the vinyl strip on the desk. And it wasn't just the shirt – it was a forest of hair beneath the shirt! And it hurt! I never knew Super Glue could hurt that much. Even a gentle tug felt like fifty Band Aids being ripped off at once.

If this has never happened to you then you might not appreciate the many sundry thoughts that go through your mind when you glue your belly to a desk. It was a Saturday afternoon. If I didn't escape, I might not be found until Monday morning. The firehall was next door. I thought about calling them. But I couldn't reach my phone. Besides, I worried that the Amherst Bee headline would read, "Williamsville Patent Attorney Glues Himself to a Desk!"

I thought about my wife and daughter, and our two dogs. I wondered if I would ever see them again.

I thought about the spectacle that would happen in our office when everyone found me on Monday morning. I have an image to uphold after all. Not to brag, but I have a degree in engineering with honors. I am admitted to practice law in four different jurisdictions. I have a measured IQ of 142 and scored a 98 on the Iowa Test of Basic Skills in fourth grade. I can solve a Rubik's Cube in fourteen seconds! But none of that mattered. I was glued to a desk. My epitaph would surely read, "Here lies an attorney who glued himself to a desk in the middle of a pandemic. RIP"

It was time to put every ounce of my engineering education and experience to work. I slowly and carefully peeled my shirt from the desk, dabbing with Goo Gone along the way. It took ten minutes to break free. But my shirt was still glued to my belly. I tried to remove my shirt to no avail. You don't really appreciate how much a button-down dress shirt weighs until it is tugging on a three-inch by one-inch strip of your belly, and all that that entails. I couldn't pull it away. I'm not saying it hurt as much as childbirth does, but maybe as much as an appendix removal without anesthesia.

It was then that I made the sacrifice. I pulled some scissors from the desk drawer and started to snip away at the shirt. I was happy that it was only a Jos. A. Bank shirt and not one of my prized Brooks Brothers Egyptian cotton Oxford button-downs. That would have been more than I could bear. The pressure was on. I had a 7 p.m. dinner reservation to keep. I cut all around the stuck portion of the shirt. When the operation was complete, I held my shirt in my hand and looked down to see a swatch of light blue end-on-end fabric stuck to my belly three inches northeast of my navel.

I won't bore you with the final details related to the removal except to say that some ouches, a few screams, and my Braun electric razor were involved.

And, when it was done, there I was, topless in my office building on a Saturday afternoon. I looked around for a shirt or a jacket, but none was to be found. I had left my jacket in the back seat of my car, and my car was in the parking lot next to the funeral home. It's not illegal for a guy to walk topless across a funeral home parking lot in Williamsville in October, but I can tell you now from experience that it doesn't feel normal either. You tend to get looks from passers-by.

I debated telling my wife about this experience. But a Bourbon Old Fashioned helps to erase Super Glue memories. So, after clicking glasses to celebrate another week of being together, she asked me, "What did you do at the office today, dear?"

"I fixed our new tenant's desk. I hope he likes it!"

The Tie and
the Paper Shredder

It's not that it was the most expensive tie I ever bought, but it wasn't cheap either. It wasn't the Brooks Brothers Golden Fleece 7-fold Satin Tie (retail $225). That tie only comes in purple so my wife would be mad at me for two reasons if I ever bought and wore that tie. But it wasn't the Brooks Brothers Signature Tartan Tie either (retail $79.50). Nope, it wasn't either of those ties that I tied around my neck on that September morning in 2002. It was the Brooks Brothers Gold Dot Rep Tie (retail $98.50).

I loved that tie. I always wore it with my Hart Schaffner & Marx charcoal suit and Allen Edmonds chili Walton shoes. Chili shoes don't match a charcoal suit, but I didn't care. I think chili shoes look spectacular with a gold tie with black dots. It was a football kind of weather day, warm but crisp with an autumn breeze. I asked my wife the same question I ask her every workday morning before leaving for the office, "Do I look like a lawyer, dear?" She just smiled.

I didn't really have to ask her. It always made me feel

like a lawyer when I wore that tie. It's not that I didn't give good legal advice when I didn't wear the Gold Dot. It's that I wrote the best patent applications when I did.

Now, not many people outside of my immediate family know this, but I am not allowed to talk about what I do at the office every day between the hours of 9 a.m. to 5 p.m. Nope! It's top-secret stuff. I am bound by no fewer than three codes of professional conduct and ethics. I see all kinds of very cool and exciting inventions from some of the most creative minds on the planet. But I can't talk about it. I can't tell you about it. I can't tell my barber about it. I can't tell my doctor about it. And I can't tell my dogs about it. It's only after the patents on those inventions have issued that I can tell you about the Silver Bullet yo-yo that I patented for a client back in the 1990s. That yo-yo went into outer space on the Space Shuttle! I'm sure you can appreciate why I had to be hush-hush for a few years about all the tricks that that yo-yo could do!

So, it should come as no surprise that we have always had a high-speed, super-duper, three-phase, 100 horsepower, titanium blade, industrial-grade shredder in the top-secret, classified document room in our law firm. You can't get into that room without a retina scan, fingerprint scan, and the ability to enter your Social Security number backwards into a keypad. The door is guarded by a dog too, although she sleeps a lot and wags her tail at everyone. There are no windows in that room which is in an undisclosed location within our building. There are motion detectors inside this soundproof room too.

It was 11:45 a.m. when the phone rang on that Tuesday morning. It was my brother, Mike. I had just finished writing one of the most important patent applications of my life. I couldn't talk about it then, but I can say now that it had to do with airport security. It made me proud to be a patent attorney. I had just finished reading the paper document when Mike asked, "Are you up for a Ted's hot dog?"

I don't know any true-blue Buffalonian who isn't always up for a Ted's charcoal-grilled hot dog, with onion rings and a chocolate milkshake.

"I'll be right there, Mike!" I exclaimed as I grabbed my patent application and headed for the document shredder room. My mouth was watering, and my stomach was grumbling as I fed the first of ninety-seven pages into the auto-feeder. The machine sucked in the first fifty-seven pages when my phone rang. It was my brother asking about my ETA.

And then it happened …

As I bent over to answer my phone, I watched in horror as the tip of my Brooks Brothers Gold Dot Rep Tie followed page fifty-seven into the titanium jaws of the shredder! My neck was suddenly pulled downward. Inch by inch I descended. I pulled back but to no avail. I screamed for help, but the room was sound-proof! No one could hear me. In case you are wondering if your whole life flashes before you as you are about to be shredded, I can tell you that it doesn't. But you do search frantically for scissors to cut your prized tie, and you do wonder if you will ever enjoy another hot dog! I also remember wondering what James Bond would do in this situation. It is at this precise moment that it came to me. I unplugged the machine. I gently pulled my tie out of the shredder.

As I left the document room I was greeted by my caring brother and all of my colleagues. My Gold Dot Rep Tie looked like cooked spaghetti. My brother immediately broke into laughter and exclaimed, as only a younger brother could, "You flaming idiot!"

I removed my tie and tossed it into the trash can.

"Oh no, you don't!" Mike remarked, as he retrieved it from the can, "I can't wait to show this to mom."

Silver Dollar Pancakes

It's not really about the pancakes, as mouth-watering as they are. The restaurant menu tries to please everyone. There are buckwheat pancakes with butter and maple syrup. There are buttermilk pancakes the size of flying disks. There are sourdough flapjacks inspired by the Klondike gold rush in Alaska. There are 49'er flapjacks from the Mother Lode Country – those are "plate-sized" and served with whipped butter and syrup. I'm not sure what gold miners and gold rushes have to do with pancakes. I've never searched for gold myself, but I might have had I known there were pancakes in the mine.

There are authentic lacy Swedish pancakes served with lingonberries and whipped butter. I've been to Sweden where I enjoyed milk and ice cream made from oats in Malmö, but I've only tasted lingonberries on Main Street in Williamsville. Lingonberries dazzled my taste buds – first sour and tart, but then sweet. I don't think they are as dazzling as the Queen's mulberries from her garden at Buckingham Palace, but I wouldn't know. I like to think that Queen Elizabeth knows her berries.

There are blueberry pancakes – really just buttermilk pancakes stuffed with plump juicy sweet blueberries. That's a match made in heaven if you ask me.

There are bacon pancakes that have a crunch – bits of bacon amid the batter. I guess bacon goes with everything and people must love these, but they are not for me. I like my bacon crisp – even burnt like a marshmallow over a campfire suits me just fine. But not in pancakes. Nope. But I might try chocolate covered bacon – as long as the chocolate was dark and the bacon was crisp.

There are banana pancakes made with – well – bananas, and dusted with powdered sugar. And there are Hawaiian pancakes served with sugar-dusted diced pineapple. Funny – I won't eat ham without pineapple, but I think I would enjoy a Hawaiian pancake.

Coconut pancakes are not an option for me. My wife just won't have a coconut in the same room with her. She lets me get away with a pina colada now and then, as long as I sip it through a straw and don't blow her coconut kisses.

There are wheat germ pancakes too. I imagine athletes and fitness buffs must eat wheat germ pancakes. I like wheat but I don't care much for germs. I can't imagine intentionally putting a germ in my mouth, even if it was drenched in maple syrup.

And, of course, there are potato pancakes on the menu, served with sour cream and cinnamon apple sauce. I think it is a stretch to call them pancakes, but they are flat and delicious. They are a family favorite. They inspire pleasant memories for me. Chef Emeril Lagasse cooked for my family and me on national TV in New York City. He invited us to the Emeril Live National Potato Recipe Contest awards show. We didn't win the contest, but he served us Swedish potato pizza made by a nice lady from Minnesota. She said it was a pizza, but it tasted like a pancake to me. Emeril even took our nine-year-old daughter into his kitchen and gave her an ice cream bar from his freezer during a commercial.

But I digress. It's not really about the pancakes. And it's not about the syrup either. My friends and family know how I feel about maple syrup. It is my most favorite food on planet Earth. I won't eat artificial syrup. I am a maple syrup snob and proud of it. I carry a bottle of pure maple syrup with me into any restaurant that might not have it. And I don't hide it. If they ask, and they usually don't, I tell them that I am allergic to artificial syrup but that I would pay them ten extra dollars for an ounce of the real stuff. I am very good at lying to restaurant servers. I want to inspire them to carry the nectar of maple trees. Yep, my fridge is always stocked with pure maple syrup from New York, Vermont, and Canada. I especially like the syrup infused with bourbon that my daughter gave me for Christmas.

The truth is, I'm really more of a crepe man than a

pancake kind of guy. I can make crepes from scratch myself. I own a crepe pan and can do them over a fire or electric burner. There is just something special and delicate about a crepe stuffed with strawberries and topped with fresh whipped cream. My crepes are as delicate as the first kiss when you know you are in love.

I'm not particular about the crepes at the Original Pancake House. I love the strawberry crepes and order them often. I don't even mind that they bring them to the table with strawberry syrup instead of my beloved maple. I love the French crepes because they remind me of my mom. And speaking of French, who doesn't love a good crepe Suzette.

I've only tried the Cherry Kijafa crepes once, and only because the menu listed them with a question – "Are they a Danish favorite?" I think a restaurant should generally do their own research and answer these types of questions themselves, but I appreciate their honesty and I tried to help. I told our server that I've been to Denmark and enjoyed crepes in Copenhagen, but I don't remember them having Montmorency cherries simmered in Kijafa sauce and lightly dusted with powdered sugar, like the ones on their menu. She seemed puzzled as I explained in detail. I don't think she knew about the question on their menu. My wife just smiled and told me, "You know you have totally become your father, don't you?"

Pancakes and syrup aside, my new most favorite

crepe is the Continental. I enjoyed them last night with my dear friend and chess coach, Barry. They are delicate crepes rolled with sour cream tempered with Triple Sec, lightly dusted with powdered sugar and served with hot tropical syrup. If you bump into me at the Pancake House, nine times out of ten I will be enjoying some Continental crepes. I don't know what continent they are from. They make me feel European, but they also remind me of a Schwinn Continental ten-speed bicycle I owned as a kid. I also ordered a large glass of cold skim milk with my crepes. I like to dine healthy!

But it's not about the crepes. It's not about the pancakes. And it's not about the syrup.

I am a "close my eyes and point to an item on the menu" kind of husband. But my dear wife always orders the same thing. She never waivers. She is as solid and reliable as the North Star. That's just one reason I love her so. She always orders the Dollar Pancakes. And they are not just any Dollar Pancakes. They are really miniature buttermilk pancakes. But they are bigger than silver dollars. And that's just one thing that makes them special. There is one thing more. There are ten of them, or so they say. The menu says it clearly, "Ten delicious silver dollar pancakes served with whipped butter and hot syrup." I think it is admirable that a restaurant tells you exactly how many pancakes they are going to bring to your table, but I feel sorry for the poor cook in the kitchen who has to cook and count at the same time.

I am not sure how many people actually count the pancakes on their plate upon delivery. But I am a pancake-counting kind of guy. My wife counts too. She is an accountant. Counting is one of the many things she is very good at. I love her for that. I, myself, have a burning desire to know how many people in the restaurant on a busy Saturday morning are counting their pancakes. I brought a little notebook with me last Saturday and wanted to go ask everyone if they were counting but my wife stopped me cold, "You are acting like your father again, dear. You have BECOME your father. Now sit down and enjoy your breakfast." I loved my father, but I love my wife more, so I sat down.

And then it happened ...

The server brought my three Continental crepes, flavored with triple sec and served with tropical syrup. She laid the plate of silver dollar pancakes in front of my wife.

Let the counting begin. There should be ten.

1, 2, 3 ... 4, 5, 6 ... 7, 8, 9, ... 10 ...

11! ... 12!

"She brought me twelve!" my wife exclaims. "She brought me a whole dozen!"

They always do. They always bring her twelve. And

she gets so genuinely excited about it every time. She is like a kid in a candy store. I tell her that they brought her twelve pancakes because she is special, and she knows I mean it.

And then it happens …

She flashes the biggest, broadest smile in the whole restaurant, in the whole darn village! It's the smile I fell in love with so many years ago. It's the smile that comes from the simple things, like a text message from our daughter, from me acting like my father, from a server who brings her more pancakes than she ordered, and from silver dollar pancakes that are bigger than silver dollars. It's the smile of love.

It's not about the pancakes. It's about the smile. It's about love.

Godiva Chocolates and the Honeymoon

It's not every day that you get married. And it's not every day that you get married at the end of your first month of law school. And it's certainly not every day that you get married at the end of your first month of law school knowing that you were admitted to law school just a month before your wedding – and so you know that you were the 285th and final student admitted to your law school class.

Imagine the emotions swirling around in your head. On the one hand (your left) you are now unemployed, having resigned from a nice paying job as an engineer. On the other hand (your right) you are about to start studying to be a lawyer. On the left hand, you now know that you are quite possibly the dumbest law student in your class, or so it seems. On the right hand, you are marrying your best friend, the love of your life, and the most beautiful woman you have ever known.

With emotions swirling and the wedding

approaching, with everything planned for the special day, there is just one more thing to plan.

"Where should we go on our honeymoon?" she asked.

I already knew the answer. I think she knew too. All of our friends had warned us. It's just not wise to make too many life changes at once. Don't quit your job and get married at the same time. Don't get married and start law school at the same time. Don't have a baby and start graduate school at the same time. Don't eat an apple fritter on your way to the gym. But we did it anyway. I quit my job, started law school, ate an apple fritter, and got married within a span of thirty days.

"I'm sorry sweetie, but I don't think we can go on a honeymoon, at least not right after the wedding. I've got tort cases to read, criminal law statutes to memorize, and Supreme Court decisions to review. And I'm not the brightest kid in the class."

"I understand," she said with a smile. "We'll go someplace warm when you finish your first semester." I smiled too. I knew then that I was marrying a woman as beautiful on the inside as on the outside.

I learned two important lessons on our wedding day. The first is that a groom should not rely on a groomsman to pick him up and give him a ride to the church (you might not make it to the church on time if he forgets to pick you up.) The second is that it is always a good idea for a man and a woman to wear a black tuxedo and white wedding dress in a car when crossing the Lewiston-Queenston Bridge into Canada.

It turns out that, if you are a properly attired couple with proper identification, not only will the Canadian Customs Officers not charge you to enter their country, but they will turn on all the flashing lights and alarms at all the toll booths and all the officers and toll-takers will come out and applaud as you drive through! I wonder if those toll-takers and officers knew that they were creating a special memory on that evening of our wedding that would last a lifetime!

And so it was that we delayed our honeymoon in favor of a weekend at the Prince of Wales hotel at Niagara-on-the-Lake and a couple of days in Toronto. The honeymoon would have to wait.

And then it happened ...

The six-hour final examination on tort law was history. So was the eight-hour exam on constitutional law. So was the four-hour exam on real property law. And I handed in my twenty-four-hour take home exam on criminal law five days before Christmas. It was time for celebrating. It was time for a honeymoon.

Like many newlyweds we didn't have much money to spend on an exotic honeymoon. My new wife had married an unemployed law student. Our options were limited.

We chose Florida, in January. Just a week. Disney World and Epcot. But first, a few days on the east coast. Mother-in-law to the rescue!

"I have some friends who have a condo – the Bennetts. He and his wife won't be using it in January. They will be here in February. I've already asked them, and they would love to give you a wedding gift of a few days in their condo," she said.

It was a beautiful place with a view of Lake Worth. We could only have dreamed of staying in a place like this. How sweet of the Bennetts. We hadn't even met them and yet they offered their place. We settled right in and made ourselves at home.

When Ellen wasn't looking, I opened the fridge and there it was – a half-eaten box of Godiva chocolates! Nobody will miss just one, I thought, as I enjoyed a dark-chocolate caramel.

When I wasn't looking, Ellen opened the fridge. Nobody will miss just one, she must have thought, as she enjoyed a buttercream.

I bought groceries on our second day. I made a picnic breakfast and set the alarm. I had never seen the sun rise over the ocean. Ellen hadn't either. It seemed like a romantic thing to do. By 6 a.m. we were on the beach – just the two of us. By 6:15 we were atop the lifeguard tower, sipping our coffee and enjoying fresh fruit and pastries, huddled under a blanket.

Sometime around 7 a.m. the sun rose over the ocean. It started as just a small sliver of orange in the east. It rose quickly and glistened with rays of red, yellow, and orange – a little purple too. In just a few minutes it was a glowing sphere warming our faces. Even though we had been married a few months, this beginning of a new day on a beach on the ocean felt like the beginning of our married life.

It was then that I asked her …

"Sweetie, have you been eating any of the chocolates in the Godiva box in the Bennetts' fridge?"

She hesitated for just a few seconds and answered …

"Have you?"

It was then that I realized that I had not only married the most beautiful woman on the planet, but also the smartest.

"Yes dear, I have."

"Me too."

"You know sweetie, there are only three chocolates left in the box. We both ate almost a half a box."

"What should we do – they gave us their condo to use – we can't leave them with an empty box of chocolates in their fridge!"

This wouldn't be the first problem we would fret about in our married life, nor our last. And it certainly wouldn't be the most important issue we would try to resolve as best we could. We talked about it all the way home from the beach.

And then we did it …

We grabbed the Godiva chocolate box and went shopping. There was no internet and no Google to search back then so we just visited store after store trying to find one that sold Godiva chocolates. It took us half a day. But alas, we found the store. We found the chocolates. We found the exact same box!

And then it happened …

We opened the box back at the condo. We both struggled to remember which chocolates were missing when we first arrived. We enjoyed such a lively discussion about pecan caramels, dark almond oysters, hazelnut crunch and dark chocolate raspberry. We racked our brains to try and remember who had eaten what. I learned then that Ellen doesn't like nuts. She never has. I love nuts. She prefers milk chocolate. I prefer dark chocolate. And I suppose that's what makes a marriage work! We spent about an hour carefully removing the chocolates that were missing before we arrived and ate the rest.

We left the Bennetts a thank you note on the kitchen counter and a half-eaten box of Godiva chocolates in their fridge. Somehow, we were too embarrassed to let them know we had enjoyed their chocolates. We laugh about it now. How silly we were. How immature.

I never met the Bennetts in person. If I ever did I would tell them this story and then hand them a brand-new unopened box of Godiva chocolates.

You know, Forrest Gump was right, "Life is like a box of chocolates. You never know what you're gonna get." I like to think the Bennetts gave us one of the best wedding gifts of all – a beautiful memory!

Dinner Reservations and
My Algebra Teacher

I can't wait! My wife and I are going out to dinner with my junior high school algebra teacher and junior varsity football coach in a few weeks. It's been about fifty years since I last sat in Mr. Joe Rizzo's classroom, but I can still hear his crystal-clear voice telling my classmates and me, "Whatever you do to the left-hand side of the equation you have to do the right-hand side!" He only had to tell me once, but he had to tell my good friend Louie pretty much every day in the ninth grade!

I'm hoping my teacher remembers me. I'm hoping he remembers how smart I used to be. Most of all, I'm hoping he can tell my wife that I really did score a perfect 100 on the 1970 June Regents Algebra Exam. She doesn't believe me! I showed her my high school transcript. She doesn't believe me! I solved a quadratic equation over pancakes at Londa's Diner in Depew last Sunday - right in front of her! She doesn't believe me! Help me Coach!!

But I digress. My teacher's wife just messaged me to let me know she made the dinner reservation for the four of us. I can't describe how happy I was to hear this – and how relieved. I thanked her for making the reservation. I told her that I wasn't very skilled at making dinner reservations.

And then it happened …

She told me that her husband usually makes ALL of their dinner reservations!

What?! Did I mishear her? How can that be?! I have not made a dinner reservation in thirty-seven years of marriage. I don't think I know how! I don't think I've ever made a dinner reservation on the telephone! Ever!

This man, this husband, this father, this teacher, this coach – was one of my idols growing up. He taught me more than he will ever know. I watched his every move on the football field and hung on his every word in the classroom. But not once, in all those junior high school days, did I ever watch him make a dinner reservation! I wonder if I was absent from school that day!

So, of course, I went straight to Google to get the straight scoop on the "Role and Responsibilities of a Husband"! I knew I was supposed to walk closest to the street when accompanying my wife on a sidewalk – so I would get splashed first. I knew I was supposed to love her unconditionally, protect her, forsake all others, be a good listener, not buy large appliances without her knowledge and consent, and never pick out paint or wallpaper for

208 Robert P. Simpson

our home. I knew I was supposed to let her toss all my bachelor clothes in a dumpster as soon as I said, "I do", and that I was never again to buy clothes on my own until I was trained (because this was in our wedding vows), but I never, ever, ever knew that I was supposed to make dinner reservations for us. How did I miss this?

It makes so much sense to me now. It is the chivalrous thing to do. It has been the case since the days of Charlemagne. Even Gautier's Ten Commandments of Chivalry, first published in 1891, which I've paraphrased, reworked, and plagiarized herebelow talks about it:

1. Thou shalt always go to church on Sunday and not pull your sister's hair in the pew.
2. Thou shalt always walk closest to the road so that you will be splashed by a horse before your beloved.
3. Thou shalt always be kind to dogs and cats.
4. Thou shalt always let your wife, daughter and all other women and girls at the table order first in a restaurant.
5. Thou shalt always walk behind your wife in a buffet line.
6. Thou shalt always make your bed without your wife having to ask you to.
7. Thou shalt never lie or fabricate the truth, unless you are a storyteller, and the true facts will put your listeners to sleep.
8. Thou shalt remain faithful to thy pledged word,

put your socks in the laundry hamper and return the toilet seat to its female preferred position.

9. Thou shalt be generous and always buy cookies from Girl Scouts and caramel corn from Boy Scouts at hardware stores.

10. Thou shalt always make dinner reservations for your wife, even if you have to do it on the telephone and can't do it online or on an app on your phone.

The sad truth is, and I have never admitted this to anyone until just now, I am afraid to make restaurant dinner reservations on the telephone. I am afraid they will reject me. I am afraid they will say, "No! You can't dine here at 6:30! Maybe we can squeeze you in at a tiny table between the restrooms and the kitchen at 9:30 if you agree to cut the stems off of haricot vert for us, but, then again, maybe we can't!" And, not to make excuses for not following Rule 10 above, but my wife is just so darn good at it! She is so sweet and kind and adorable on the phone. Restaurants never disappoint her. They never turn her down.

But tomorrow is a new day. I just might pick up the phone and call a restaurant on my own. I think I owe it to my teacher and to my wife.

Once a teacher – always a teacher! Thank you, Coach!

"Sweetie – can you help me find the phone number ...?"

I Love Ham!

I'm not finicky when it comes to food. I will eat almost anything, except for clams. I love clams. I once brought twenty dozen clams on a camping trip to Letchworth State Park with my wife. It was just the two of us. We were newlyweds. I brought a bottle of red wine, filet mignon, two lobster tails, a dozen eggs and a bag of potato chips too because I wanted my wife to enjoy camping in a tent. We had clams on a half shell, steamed clams, fried clams, and clams casino for lunch and dinner. We had clams and eggs for breakfast - every day! It is hard for two people to eat 240 clams in four days at Letchworth State Park. My wife won't go camping with me anymore.

I will eat almost anything, except for shrimp, oysters, crab, and lobster. I love shrimp, oysters, crab, and lobster. But I haven't enjoyed shrimp, oysters, crab or lobster since Christmas Eve in 2000 at my friend, Linda Case's house. My lips tingled and swelled as we drove home. I couldn't talk. My wife enjoyed it at first but then she rushed me to the hospital. The doctor asked me, "Did you by any chance eat twenty dozen clams at Letchworth

State Park with your wife when you were first married?"

"Why yes, I did! How did you know?"

"I've seen it before. Did you also feel guilty eating more than your share of shrimp cocktail at family holiday parties - you know - going back for more when you thought no one was looking?"

"Well - maybe."

"I'm sorry to tell you that you have consumed more than your lifetime allotment of shellfish. We all have a preprogrammed limit - and you have reached yours! You have a severe case of Letchworth Clamitis - probably the worst I've ever seen!"

"But I am only fifty-four! What am I to do?"

"Order Chilean seabass, close your eyes, and pretend it's lobster!"

I love Chilean seabass, but it's not lobster.

I am not a finicky eater. But I hate ham. I have always hated ham. I won't eat a ham sandwich. I won't eat ham and eggs. I won't read Dr. Suess' book about green eggs and ham. He was a fine writer but I wish he wrote about capellini instead of ham. I love capellini. I wish I was Italian.

My dad loved ham. My mom loved ham. My brother and sisters loved ham. My wife loves ham. Even my dogs love ham. I'm not finicky but I won't eat ham, unless it is covered with pineapple. If there is twice as much pineapple on my fork as ham, then I will suffer through it.

My dad cooked a ham every Easter Sunday for as long as I can remember. My dad knew I didn't like ham but he cooked a ham on my eighth birthday anyway because my birthday was on Easter Sunday. I ate it because I loved my dad and because he covered the ham with pineapple.

One time when I was forty-two my wife and I went to my mom and dad's for Easter dinner. We brought scalloped potatoes. My dad called everyone to the dinner table. That's when it happened. That's when I noticed. That's when I asked him, "Dad, where's the pineapple?"

"What pineapple?"

I loved my dad, but it turns out that it is almost impossible to buy a can of pineapple in the city of Niagara Falls on Easter Sunday. It is a lot harder to buy pineapple in my hometown on Easter Sunday than it is to buy D-cell batteries for your toys on Christmas morning. You can buy D-cell batteries at Marios at 24th Street and Pine Avenue on Christmas morning. But Mario doesn't sell pineapple - at least not on Easter Sunday.

We celebrated this past Easter at the home of longtime friends in Jupiter, Florida. When we asked what we could bring, imagine my elation when our friends replied that they would love it if we would bring a ham! I heard it with my own ears through my wife's phone on speaker.

"WE would LOVE to bring a ham!" she quickly replied. I love my wife but sometimes she has difficulty in selecting the right pronoun to use in her sentences.

"I know, I know! You won't eat ham without pineapple. I know your dad forgot to cook the ham with pineapple on Easter Sunday when you were forty-two. I know Mario's didn't sell pineapple!"

Being married for a long time to someone you love is a beautiful thing. I didn't need to say a word as she drove us to Publix to buy fresh pineapple.

And then I suffered silently outside the Honey Baked Ham store on U.S. 1 across the street from our condo, as she went inside to pick up the ham she ordered online. The place was packed! There was a security guard inside the store. Who would steal a fricking ham?! I stayed in the car. I wasn't pouting. I'm not that kind of husband. I was just daydreaming about pineapple. I love pineapple.

And then it happened ...

The ham and sides were served buffet style. I placed one slice of Honey Baked ham upon my plate and covered it with three fresh pineapple rings. We said grace and raised a glass to toast on this beautiful sacred day.

I took a bite. And then another. And then another. Then I took a bite without pineapple when no one was looking. And then another. I couldn't believe it. I am so ashamed. I LOVE Honey Baked ham! Who knew?! I went back for seconds!

"Sweetie - how long has that Honey Baked Ham store

been across the street from our condo?"

"It's been there forever, at least twenty years, before we even bought our place."

"Was their ham always this good?"

She just smiled. Married couples can sometimes say everything they need to with a smile.

I love my wife. And now I love ham.

I wonder if I love liver?

The Tale of the Polish Wengue Chess Chairs

It had four sturdy legs and a top with sixty-four squares. The light squares were inlaid, made of brewing beech wood and the dark squares were stained to resemble wengue. This was clearly the work of a skilled craftsman. Wengue is a gorgeous tropical timber, dark in color with a distinctive figure and a strong partridge wood pattern. It just screams, "Put me in a mancave!" It screams, "Play the Sicilian Defense on top of me!" It screams, "Go ahead, fianchetto your Bishops!"

I knew it wasn't real wood from the millettia laurenti legume tree from Africa. I knew that African rosewood was an endangered species. But it was beautiful, nonetheless.

I spotted it on a website of a chess shop in North Massapequa. I'd never been to North Massapequa. The table wasn't always in North Massapequa. It was made in Lubelskie, Poland, almost 5,000 miles from my mancave. I ordered it immediately and scheduled shipment during my wife's next trip out of town.

It arrived two weeks later. I carefully peeled away the bubble wrap with eager anticipation. It arrived without a scratch. It was perfect, but I polished it anyway. And then I arranged the white and black armies on those beech wood and wengue squares.

And then it happened …

It occurred to me that you really can't play a game of chess standing up. You need chairs. There were chairs in the photograph on the website. They matched the table perfectly. They were wengue with black leather covered seats. I called the shop.

"I would like to order four wengue chairs to match my wengue chess table."

"We don't have those chairs in stock."

"Can you get them from the manufacturer?"

"I don't know. We have never had them in stock."

"But they are shown on your website."

"I know. But the chairs are in Poland."

"Can you please call Poland and ask them to send you the chairs?"

"Sure."

The chairs were made by a company named Biasov. Google says the company has one employee. He must be one very talented dude. I would love to meet him –

or her! I waited two weeks for the reply. Then I called the shop.

"Did you reach the company in Poland?"

"Yes."

"What did they say?"

"They said they won't sell us the chairs."

"Why not?"

"They said the chairs are too expensive to sell?"

"How much are they?"

"They wouldn't say?"

"Did you tell them that I can't play chess standing up on account of my knee and hip replacements?"

"No, I didn't."

"Please call them back and tell them that a guy with bad knees in Buffalo doesn't care how much they cost. He needs to sit down and wants to buy them."

I waited another two weeks with no reply. I called again.

"Did you call them back?"

"Yes."

"What did they say?"

"They said they won't sell you the chairs."

"Why not?"

"They said shipping them to Buffalo from Poland would cost more than the chairs themselves."

"Thank you."

It was then that I called my dear friend, Werner

218 Robert P. Simpson

Reichert, a patent attorney in Regensburg, Germany. I knew that Werner's colleague, Monika Martel, was from Poland.

"Werner, could you please do me a favor?"

"Sure Bob, what do you need?"

"Could you please ask Monika to call the Biasov company in Lubelskie, Poland, speak to them in Polish, and buy four wengue chairs for a chess table for me? Please have them shipped to your office, and then ship them to Buffalo."

"Sure Bob – happy to do that for you."

Three days later … I received a phone call from Werner. He was having a great time laughing as he explained …

"Hi Bob, it's Werner. Monika called the company in Poland and asked to buy the chairs."

"Great! What did they say?"

"They asked if she was calling on behalf of some nut-case chess player from Buffalo who wants to buy these chairs."

"What did she say?"

"She told them 'yes' – that you are a nut-case! She told them that if they didn't sell us the chairs that you would hop on a plane to Germany and we would all drive to Poland together in a rental truck to buy the chairs."

"What did they say?"

"They asked for your shipping address!"

My four beautiful wengue chess table chairs traveled from Lubelskie, Poland to Warsaw by truck, wrapped in bubble wrap. They were flown over the Atlantic Ocean to JFK airport on Long Island. They were flown on another plane from JFK to Buffalo. They were delivered to my office when my wife was out of town. The shipping did cost more than the chairs themselves. On advice of counsel, I can't say how much the chairs cost because it is apparently one of the grounds for divorce in New York. I'm pretty sure my wife wouldn't divorce me for buying chess table chairs since I don't play golf, but she might make me sleep in the garage during January.

The chairs are beautiful. I am sure I play better chess while sitting on them. My wife and friends think I am a nut, but those wengue chairs make me feel like a Grandmaster.

I Didn't Have to
Let You Win!

Our games started more than thirty years ago. He was more than my boss, my mentor and dear friend; he was my oft-times chess partner. After teaching me patent law during the day, he would sometimes appear in the doorway of my office just before closing time, wearing a grin, and holding a bag of chessmen. "Are you ready?"

Like me, Mike was very competitive – in everything! You can't really say no to the man who gave you your first job in the practice of law; to the man who gave you a chance to stay in Western New York and build a career and raise a family when no one else did.

"Sure, Mike, set 'em up!"

As we retired to the library, our staff was leaving for the day through the front door. "They're at it again," Karen mumbled. "They'll be in that library all night!" exclaimed Linda. "I'd rather watch paint dry," moaned Pam.

Ever the sportsman, Mike would hold a black pawn in one hand behind his back, and a white pawn in the other. I always pointed to his left hand with my right. I'm not sure Mike ever figured that out, even though we've done this hundreds of times. But he is an honorable man and always shuffled the pawns behind his back before asking me to pick. Neither of us knew which color we would draw.

There is a long tradition in chess, handed down from experienced players to newbies. The game doesn't begin with the move of a piece. It begins with a handshake between friends soon to be combatants. This is followed by the starting of the clock by the person playing black, and then the movement of a white pawn or piece on the board. There is a beautiful cadence and rhythm to the start of every chess game – it is pure poetry.

It doesn't take long to get lost in blissful thought over the board. There are more possible moves in a game of chess than there are atoms in the universe. The whole world, and all of its problems and stresses, just seem to disappear as we ponder, wonder, reflect and search for that one true best move among the millions and billions of possibilities.

The truth is, I am a lousy chess player. But Mike is even lousier! I'm rated about 1500 and Mike about 1200. That might not seem like much of a difference, but it means that Mike can only expect to win about fifteen percent of our games. I'm not sure he knew that. I know I didn't. I know neither of us really cared. We just enjoyed playing each other.

It's a delicate thing to compete against your boss – the guy who signs your paycheck. On the one hand you feel like you really shouldn't beat him because if he fires you and your wife asks you why and you say it's because you checkmated him with your queen and knight, your marriage could end right then and there. On the other hand, my boss was one of the smartest people I've ever known – he's a chemist, a physicist, a patent attorney, and he wrote a gazillion patents on cancer treatments. He would know in a minute if I was throwing a game. So, I decided I had to play all out in every game.

And so it happened, we played game after game after game. I played the Ruy Lopez and the Trompowsky with the white pieces and the French Defense with black. Mike mostly played king pawn openings but sometimes he played the English. We played with a clock but never paid much attention to the time. When Mike ran out of time, which he always did, I just quietly reset the time on both clocks. He didn't seem to notice. We would play for hours.

I'm not sure I won as many games as I was supposed to, but Mike ended most of our games the same way. He would tip over his king, extend his hand, say "Congratulations!" and then inevitably exclaim, "I didn't have to let you win!"

Game after game he always said the same thing, "I

didn't have to let you win!" I would ask him "No?" And he would explain that, somewhere around move fifteen, he didn't need to let me pin his knight, or double his pawns or fork his queen and rook. Or somewhere around move twenty-four he didn't need to let me take that rook pawn. I'm not one to usually keep track of such things, but there was a stretch of sixty-seven games in a row once that Mike didn't have to let me win!

And then it happened ...

After playing 897 games that Mike didn't have to let me win, I just couldn't take it anymore. I went out and bought a sensory chess board – one of those fancy boards from the Netherlands that records every move made in a chess game and stores it on a computer. I connected the board to my laptop and hid the computer under the table in the library. Mike never noticed the cables or the computer.

I drew white and played the Trompowsky. Mike moved his knight from f6 to e4, attacking my dark square bishop on g5. He expected me to move it but instead I supported it with a pawn on h4. I learned this trick from Grand Master Julian Hodgson of England. Mike took the bait! He snatched my bishop with authority and removed it from the board. I recaptured his knight with my h-pawn, opening the h-file for an attack later in the game.

We maneuvered our pieces for the next two hours. Mike had the bishop pair, but his light square bishop was out of play for most of the game, allowing me to dominate the light squares. It was a hard-fought game, one of our best battles. It ended when Mike tipped over his king on the forty seventh move.

And then it happened, for the 898th time, after he tipped over his king and extended his hand, he told me, "I didn't have to let you win!"

"No? What do you mean?"

"I didn't have to take your dark-square bishop with my knight!"

"Which move was that, Mike? Let's set up the position and analyze it."

"I don't remember the move sequence, but it was somewhere in the opening."

It was then that I pulled the laptop out from under the table, showed Mike the recorded game, and backed it up to the position just before he took my bishop.

"Let's replay the game from here Mike, just don't take the bishop. Show me how you didn't have to let me win."

Mike is a warrior. He accepted the challenge. We played a completely new game from that spot. He didn't take my bishop. He played his pawn to d5 instead. We played that game out for another couple of hours. It ended when Mike tipped over his king on the forty third move. He extended his hand as I waited for him to speak first, "Congratulations! Nice game!"

The following week we set up the pieces again in the library. Mike drew white and pushed his pawn to e4. I gave my cherished French Defense a rest and played the Sicilian Defense in honor of my mother-in-law. Mike crushed me in thirty-six moves! I tipped over my king, extended my hand, and said, "Congratulations Mike! You played a great game! But I didn't have to let you win!"

Mike smiled, and then we both broke into a great laugh. We both knew the whole truth. We both won every time we shared a game together.

Barney and the Book

For the past twenty years our law firm has shared a parking lot with the funeral home next door. They own the lot, except for a string of spots adjacent our building. But we have an easement to park there anytime, day or night, as long as there isn't a wake or funeral in progress. I'm happy to accommodate the undertaker. He has a tough enough job without worrying about unauthorized folks parking in his lot.

For the past twenty summers, the undertaker has hired a guy to guard our shared parking lot during the Williamsville Old Home Days. He seems like a very nice man, of slender build, and diligent in his duties. He sits in his truck if it's raining and in a lawn chair if it isn't. He has a list of cars, license plates and names on a sheet of paper secured to his clipboard. If you don't have business in our office or the funeral home, he waves you away. If you get by him and you aren't on the list, he scurries across the parking lot, zigzagging around cars like George Costanza in the Seinfeld Frogger episode. He is always polite but firm as he asks people to leave our parking lot. He doesn't wear a badge. He doesn't need to. He just has that air of authority about him. He is just so darn nice and polite that decent folks won't argue with him.

For the past twenty summers, I have waved to him from my car. In our first summer, when he didn't know me, he ran over to my car; he chased me down as I tried to get into my office before he caught up. I couldn't outrun him. He asked me if I worked in "that building". I replied, "Not only do I work there, I work for my wife there." He put a checkmark on his list and allowed me to pass. That was our only spoken communication, until today.

For the past twenty summers, for four consecutive days, I have marveled at this guard's diligence. And, without fail, as I've entered my office, I have mumbled to the first few people I see, "It's going to be a good day. We are all safe. Barney Fife is on the job."

Now, I didn't mean any disrespect by my comment. I LOVE Barney Fife! I watch him daily on TV. I happen to think that Don Knotts is one of the all-time great comedic geniuses. But, there is just something about the way that our funeral home parking lot deputy goes about his daily duty that reminds me of Barney patrolling the streets of Mayberry. I just keep expecting him to make a citizen's arrest the way Gomer tried to arrest Barney for an illegal U-turn back in the 1960s.

For the past twenty summers, I never knew his real name, until today ...

And then it happened ...

I stepped outside the rear door of our building to enjoy some fresh air. I was waiting for my wife and daughter to join me to walk down the street for lunch. Barney spotted me. He came quickly across the parking lot, clipboard in hand. He was on a mission. I wondered if I had committed a funeral home parking lot infraction. To my great relief, he wasn't after me! When he came within range, he asked me if I knew the lady parked in the white sedan. He asked me if, "she was one of my mine?" I replied that I didn't know. We would have to wait until she left her car so I could get a better look and confirm her identity.

It was a bit of a wait. Barney broke the awkward silence, "Mr. Simpson," he said, "I just want to tell you how much I enjoy your My View stories in the Buffalo News!" Waves of guilt overcame me as he finished his sentence and started the next. "Yes, sir," he said, "I read that section of the paper every day, and you are one of the REGULARS! By that I mean, when I see your name and your face in the paper, I sit down with my coffee and read every word!" I felt lower than low upon hearing this. I had referred to him as "Barney Fife" at least eighty times during the past twenty years. I never asked his name. I never asked him how his day was going. I only waved as I drove by. I searched my conscience to try and figure out if my reference to him as Barney was in any way condescending.

But he interrupted my conscience searching with more kindness. "When are you going to write another article? It just makes my day!"

"That's so kind of you to say! I didn't think anybody read those amateur pieces. By the way, what is your name?"

"My name is Doug," he replied, as I introduced myself with a handshake.

Well, I just ran right down to my office, grabbed a brand-new hardcover copy of my book, inscribed it to my new friend, Doug, wished him the best in my own hand, signed my name and then walked across the parking lot to deliver it.

"I hope you enjoy the stories, Doug!"

"I'm sure I will. I'll read it this week when I'm guarding the lot. I'll let you know if I like it."

"It's going to be a good day. We are all safe. Doug is on the job."

Mr. Harper

It was a cold day in February. Graduation was a few months away. My engineering classmates and I had been taking things apart and figuring out how they worked for years. We had survived courses in differential equations, special and general relativity, and electromagnetic field theory. We had blown things up in the lab. We had worked as co-op students in industry. Some of us had even flown on a jet plane for the very first time to interview for jobs after graduation. We were looking forward to buying new Camaros and Mustangs with our first paychecks from General Electric, Eastman Kodak, Xerox, and Westinghouse.

We waited in the classroom in Kate Gleason College of Engineering for our professor to arrive. We were all suffering from "senior-itis" and looking forward to an easy course, "Patent Law for Engineers". It would be a cakewalk. He walked in wearing a dark brown three-piece suit and a tie with a perfectly symmetrical Windsor knot. He carried an old leather briefcase. He didn't look like an engineer. He didn't carry a slide rule or wear a pocket protector. He looked like a lawyer. And he was – a patent lawyer.

He began class by telling us stories about Edison, Marconi, Westinghouse, and Tesla. He told us that we would soon be inventing ourselves and we ought to know a thing or two about the patent system. He knew he had to earn our trust and respect – and he did. He explained how differential gears worked. He explained sun gears and planetary gears and that's how we knew – he was one of us. He was an engineer who happened to go to law school.

Once he had us, he moved effortlessly from mechanics to law, teaching us about novelty, obviousness, and the doctrine of equivalents. He spent a whole class on the printed matter doctrine and the case *In re Miller* about a husband who invented a special measuring cup to save his poor wife from having to do the complicated math in reducing recipes after the "kids left the nest". He told us how the judge explained that housewives weren't very good at math and Mr. Miller didn't want his wife to "trouble her pretty little head" with long division. He told us how the judge released this opinion on Christmas Eve and how his wife probably made him sleep in the garage that night. He told us stories like these to reinforce the legal stuff he was teaching us. He engaged us, each of us, from start to finish.

Ralph Harper didn't need the money. That's not

why he taught. He was Chief Patent Counsel at Gleason Works in Rochester. He taught because he loved to, and he taught because he wanted to give back. He taught because he thought engineers should know something about patents.

I fell in love with this course on the very first day. Ralph was a fantastic teacher. I was so awestruck that I would walk with him to his car after every class and I would try to time my arrival to walk into class with him too. It wasn't about "kissing up" to the teacher to gain favor in grading. It was because I wanted to learn as much as I could from him. I asked him a gazillion questions. I asked him why he took the time to teach at the college. He told me that there just might be a patent attorney in waiting in the class and he wanted to spark that interest. He told me that a teacher had sparked his interest and he wanted to pay it forward.

I got an "A" in the course. It wasn't that I was the smartest student. It was because I fell in love with the subject matter and the way Ralph taught it. I had already committed to designing polyphase induction motors for Westinghouse after graduation. But Ralph sparked an interest that just wouldn't go away.

When I told Ellen about Mr. Harper, she encouraged me to go to law school to pursue that dream. She worked to pay the bills while I studied the law.

And then it happened ...

Seven years after graduation from law school I was sitting at the airport in Washington, D.C. Across the terminal I saw an elderly gentleman, looking dapper in a brown three-piece suit, searching through papers in an old leather briefcase. He looked familiar. It was Ralph Harper. I hadn't seen him in fifteen years. I startled him when I asked, "Mr. Harper?" He looked up and replied, "Yes?"

I introduced myself and asked him if he remembered me. He told me he did. He told me he couldn't forget the student who walked with him to his car after every class he taught in the spring of 1979. He asked me what I was doing in Washington. I told him that I was a patent attorney and doing some patent searching at the Patent Office. He told me that he was there to argue a case with an Examiner. I told him I still remembered *In re Miller* and that clever measuring cup.

I told him I became a patent attorney because he sparked an interest that just wouldn't go away. He flashed a broad smile. I thought I saw a tear forming in his eye. I know a tear was forming in mine. I asked him how many of his former students went on to become patent lawyers. He told me, "One that I know of!" We shook hands and I thanked him for teaching. He headed for his gate to catch his flight to Rochester, and I headed to mine to catch my flight to Buffalo. No point in two grown men tearing up in an airport.

Ralph passed away a few years ago. When I saw his obituary, I wrote a note to his daughters to let them know how much he affected my life. I let them know that I actually teach some of the same cases in my law school course that Ralph taught me at RIT. I could teach more recent cases, but the ones Ralph taught me are still good law, so I teach them for Ralph. I even bring the *In re Miller* measuring cup into class and tell the story. I don't tell the story half as well as Ralph did. But I try my best.

Mia

She doesn't need to be told it's bedtime. We don't need to ask her. She waits until we sit on the edge of the bed. She prances over, hops a few inches into the air, bouncing on her hind legs and reaching up to us with her front paws, trusting us completely to scoop her up, catch her in midair, not let her fall, and toss her gently on the comforter atop our bed. Good day or bad, she senses our mood and cuddles between us. Her tail always wags. She is always happy. She is never sad.

We wonder what she knows, how she feels and what she is thinking as she rests her chin upon our arm or leg, with those beautiful brown eyes begging for attention. "Cuteness alert, cuteness alert!" we whisper as we quickly look for our phones to capture the moment in a photo before she moves. It's crazy really; we have thousands of photos of her on our phones, but we always think her latest pose is the cutest ever.

She is one of those Shelties who begs you to pet her. But as you reach for her ears or the top of her head, she ducks and spins and flips onto her back, inviting a belly rub instead. And when we indulge, because we just can't resist, she scratches her nose with her front two paws, first the left, then the right, back and forth, back and forth, in sync with her wagging tail - another "cuteness alert".

It's the darndest thing, this Sheltie of ours. A few minutes of tickling her belly and her eyes start to close, her tail slows down, as she drifts off to sleep, and dreams of treats and tennis balls. They say that dogs who sleep on their backs are letting you know that they feel secure in their home – that they totally trust their humans. She is most vulnerable when on her back with her four paws reaching for heaven, but she knows that she is safe – she is our little angel.

We drift off ourselves before too long. There is just something soothing about a sleeping puppy that makes you forget about your troubles. Our Sheltie comforts us with her trust and love. She gives us oh so much more than we can ever repay.

And then it happens ...

It can happen at 4, or 5 or 6 a.m. We cross that line from sleep to wake. The line is hazy and not well defined. We open one eye but dare not move. The bathroom calls but we dare not move. The birds are chirping but we dare not move. We don't even roll from side to back or back to side. We just pretend that we are still asleep.

But she is too smart. She knows. We don't know how she knows but she does. She walks over and stares at us. We know she is there, but we don't dare open our eyes. It is just TOO EARLY. "Go away," we think but really don't mean. She waits a minute, maybe two, and then she gives us a gentle kiss or pokes us with her paw.

The jig is up. She knows we are awake. As we open our eyes she bolts to the edge of the bed. She leaps to the floor before our heads leave our pillows. She runs to the counter as excited as a kid on Christmas morning. As we open the cupboard she starts to hop. She seems more like a rabbit than a dog, leaping a foot into the air, over and over, trying to watch us fill her dish with her daily breakfast. It is such a mystery that a dog can get so excited over kibbles and bits of food. She acts as if she hasn't eaten in days.

She puts it all into perspective, really, this puppy of ours. All you really need is a warm bed, a belly rub, a little food, water, and love.

MRIs and an Itchy Nose

At my age, every now and then, a doctor decides that he should take a closer look inside of me to find out how, exactly, I am still standing and breathing. That happened to me today. X-rays are one thing, but "magnetic resonance imaging" is quite another. The whole phrase just rolls off your tongue so easily that I don't know why anyone would use the abbreviation. Sometimes at cocktail parties, I try to inject these words into normal conversation just to sound smart and impressive. "What did you do today?" I hope someone will ask, just so I can reply, "I was imaged with magnetic resonance."

I was so excited about having an MRI that I asked my wife to drive me so I could focus on the experience. After all, it's not every day that hydrogen nuclei in our bodies are first gripped by powerful magnetic fields, and then stimulated into producing radio waves. I was wondering what kind of radio waves my body organs would produce. I was hoping for rock and roll but pretty sure I would emit easy listening. I explained the operating theory of the machine to my wife in the waiting room as she adjusted her Bose noise-canceling headphones.

If you've never experienced an MRI and want to know what it's all about, let me explain. There are academic debates over who really invented the giant magnetic imaging tool, but I have my own theory. I think it was Dr. Oscar Mayer. Think about it. Doesn't the machine sort of look like an upside-down hot dog bun, where you are the hot dog? And those aren't normal Pepperidge Farms hot dog rolls surrounding your body as you lay prone and helpless, strapped to a stretcher with only an inch of headroom between you and giant coils of wire. Those rolls are going to pepper you with 1.5 to 3.0 Teslas of magnetic energy, or, in plain English, about 5000 Gauss! That's a lot of Gauss!

But it's all pretty safe, as long as you pay attention and carefully answer all the questions on the clipboard carefully designed to determine if you have any ferromagnetic material in your body, and don't try to sneak your cell phone or your wristwatch inside the human torpedo tube with you. Those are serious questions, and you need to pay attention. You DO NOT want to be the guy who breaks the $6 million machine and has to have his wrist and wristwatch surgically removed from the inner wall of the MRI tube when they turn on the magnets.

Once you are in your blue MRI pajamas and interrogated about not bringing any metal into the imaging room, your host and MRI specialist greets you with a single question, "Hi, I'm Sue, I'll be imaging you today. Are you claustrophobic?" This seemed like an odd way to start a conversation, so I simply replied, "Hi Sue, I'm Bob, are you arachnophobic?" I don't even know if that is a real word, but I wanted to engage her on her level. I can discuss phobias intelligently with anybody.

Sue was very nice, and very concerned about my comfort while she prepared to send 5000 Gauss of magnetic energy through my soft tissue. I'm an electrical engineer so I was empathetic and played along as she asked me what kind of music I enjoyed. It puzzled me that she asked me this question as she handed me earplugs and noise-blocking headphones. "easy listening," I replied.

And then the chit-chat sadly came to a close, and I was loaded into the human torpedo tube, with the magnetic hot dog bun all around me. The Eagles "Hotel California" came blaring through the room and I started to bob my head to the music when Sue's commanding voice came loudly through the loudspeaker, "Don't move! Your first scan will start in ten seconds, and last for four minutes."

I froze in obedience to Sue's voice. I certainly didn't want to mess up the magnets. Who knew what those things could do to my spleen? I wondered what she meant, exactly, by the phrase, "Don't move!" I'm a literal person, so I decided I should hold my breath.

I sensed that I was turning blue around the one-minute mark, but I was determined not to move, and not to breathe. My cheeks puffed up and I grimaced to hold it in. At two minutes I couldn't take it anymore and let it all out. Uh oh! Did I screw it up? Was Sue watching me? Did I move when I exhaled? Did I mess up the image? I came in for an image of my hip – what if my doctor thinks I have a broken nose?

And then the sounds started. I closed my eyes as the magnets started to buzz, pulse and pound. I was listening to Diamond Girl by Seals and Crofts during the next scan. The magnets started off in a sinusoidal rhythm totally out of sync with Diamond Girl. It got better when Stevie Nicks and Fleetwood Mac serenaded me with Rhiannon as the waves bombarded my sacroiliac joint. It was a mono-channel sound, and I couldn't pinpoint its source. At first it was near my toes. Then the sounds tickled my kneecap and traveled up my femur. Then a bass drum pounded my buttocks. Oh no! All of a sudden it sounded like machine gun fire, and I thought I was under attack. But just then, Sue's calming voice came on again, "Congratulations, you're done with your second scan. Your next scan will take five minutes."

I felt happy when Sue congratulated me for how well I was being scanned, but then I wondered what may have happened to the poor fellows who couldn't hold their breath as long as I could. Can you actually fail an MRI test?

There's really not much to do when you're being scanned, and your mind starts to wander. Well, at least my mind started to wander. I started to wonder and imagine what kind of animal or machine might make the sounds I was hearing. I swear I heard a hippopotamus gasping for air. Then there was a horse whinnying. I swear I heard Ringo Starr manning the drums for an entire scan of my lower vertebrae. Then there was the annoying pig, "Oink, oink, oink, oink … oink, oink, oink, oink!" for three straight minutes as I dreamed of bacon. I wanted to shoot that pig and roast him over an open fire. I heard the honk, honk, honk, honk, honk of a 1966 Studebaker. But it was a broken horn and just wouldn't shut off. Just when I thought I recognized the animal making the next sound it disappeared, and an entirely new sound hit me from a completely different direction.

At eight minutes into the scan, as you are trying your best to remain perfectly still, something happens to every single person who is ever scanned in an MRI machine. It's the "itch." And it is always on your nose. You feel it and start to wonder. "Can I scratch it?" "Will Sue notice?" It itches so bad, and you really, really, really want to scratch it but you can't. You have this silly thought, "Can I twitch my nose and make it go away?" "Will Sue be mad at me if I twitch my nose?" "Is twitching your nose 'moving' in violation of the MRI Official Rules of Conduct?" You start to wonder if you really have an itch, or if it is imaginary. You get so focused on your itch, that you don't even notice that, suddenly, the magnets are playing a bass note completely in rhythm with Proud Mary by Creedence Clearwater Revival.

I admit that I even started to wonder what these magnetic waves were doing to my body, and how much personal information I was conveying to my MRI specialist in the other room. I had this fearful image in my head of Sue pointing to a screen and sharing information with her co-worker, "Look – he had a Mighty Taco for lunch and an apple empanada for dessert." I really didn't want my orthopedic surgeon to have this information. He wanted me to lose some weight!

As I was enjoying this cacophony of magnetic sounds, I started to wonder what my wife was doing in the waiting room. I lost all sense of time listening to this symphony and started to worry that our dogs were hungry at home. I wanted to get a message to her but couldn't. There is no intercom in an MRI machine. I know – I checked.

Speaking of time, I knew Sue was trying to be helpful, but she kept telling me how long my next scan would take, and then the next, and then the next. "Your next scan will last four minutes … Your next scan will last three minutes … Your next scan will be a long one – six minutes!" I tried my best to remember these scan times, in the order that Sue was announcing them. I wanted to write down the times for future reference, but I didn't have a pencil, and my arms were strapped to my side. I couldn't help but wonder exactly what I was supposed to do with this information. I feared there might be a test at the end. I was really hoping she would tell me, "This whole thing will take an hour, so there is plenty of time for your wife to go home and feed your dogs." But this never happened.

After fifty minutes in the tube, Sue announced the final scan. I braced for impact. The final scan was nothing short of amazing. The magnets started with a slow drumroll in stereo and then increased in amplitude and frequency. John Philip Sousa resonated in the tube with a marching song from a parade. Then Led Zeppelin and the Allman Brothers joined forces for the climax. Magnets were firing from all directions in Dolby 7.1 Surround Sound, just like the fireworks finale on the 4th of July. Sue was just showing off now. Boy could she play an electromagnetic tune. I could feel my internal body organs respond to all that energy – I knew my images would be magnificent and my doctor would be pleased. It was glorious, so glorious I almost accidentally moved my toes.

And then it happened …

The machine shut down, the concert ended, and Sue announced that I was done. She flipped a switch, and a conveyor belt moved my body out of the tube. I raised my hand and slowly extended my finger to scratch my nose. But the itch was gone. So I went home with my wife to feed our dogs.

Physical Therapy and Bumper-Walkers

Betty showed up at my home three days after my discharge from the hospital. I came home with a sparkling new ceramic and titanium left hip and, as best I could tell, it was her job to make sure that the pain I was experiencing in the hospital would continue at the same level in the comfort of my own home.

She was a tall woman from Poland, about six inches taller than me. She was very athletic, captain of the Polish national tennis team, very kind and very knowledgeable about how replacement body parts work. She explained to me, for example, that the only difference between 10w30 and 5w30 oils is that a 10w30 oil will move slower than a 5w30 oil during cold startups. At operating temperatures, both oils will have the same viscosity (30) and will flow and protect identically. This is important information that I will remember when I oil my new hip joint.

I did everything Betty told me to do, partly because she was taller and stronger than me, partly because she pointed my cane at me while supervising my exercises, but mostly because she understood how a body is supposed to work and I didn't. She explained, for example, that I should not cross my legs, tie my shoes, put on socks, or bend more than ninety degrees, as these things could dislocate my hip. My wife bought me a protractor and Birkenstock's for my birthday, so I am all set. I gave up wearing socks and tie shoes for Lent and I measure my body angles every hour and record them in a daily log.

Betty and I did exercises everywhere in my home while my dogs barked at us. We started in a chair where I showed her that I could curl my feet at my ankles. I could also swirl them around in circles. I wasn't sure why this was good for my hip, but she seemed pleased that I could do these things with my feet. Then we went to the kitchen where I showed her that I could walk sideways to the left and to the right while holding onto the counter and making a chocolate milkshake in my blender at the same time.

Physical therapists insist that all exercises be done in two sets of ten, but they don't count out loud and seem annoyed if you do. Worse, they insist on carrying on a conversation with you while you are trying to count your sideways leg lifts silently to yourself. They pretend like they are counting but they really aren't. I didn't tell her, but I have the ability to recite the entire Gettysburg Address while doing exactly 147 jumping jacks, so I never lost count. I hope the exact number of exercises doesn't matter because I did fifteen repetitions of everything instead of ten so I would get better sooner.

It was hard to remember all the different exercises Betty wanted me to do on the days she didn't come to my house. To help me, she gave me sheets of paper with pictures of old people sitting in chairs doing exercises while watching Rachel Ray and Medicare commercials on TV. It seemed strange to do all this during the day when folks my age were at the office working, so I watched the Andy Griffith show instead.

I quickly became bored with her exercises so the next time she came over I showed her two of my own. First, I showed her that I could rub my belly with my left hand while tapping the top of my head with my right hand at the same time. She seemed intrigued so I had her practice that exercise for ten minutes while I made a cup of coffee. When I returned, I showed her my all-time favorite exercise. I held my hands in front of me with my right and left index fingers pointed at one another and one inch apart. Then I slowly started drawing clockwise circles in the air with my right hand. Once that got going, I started drawing counterclockwise circles of the same diameter at the same time with my left hand. She was both mesmerized and impressed by my athletic prowess. After our session I watched her in her car in my driveway trying to spin her hands in circles in opposite directions.

She sat there for twenty minutes but just couldn't do it. Her hands just kept following one another in clockwise circles. She drove away flustered. I think that's why she fired me.

Two days later, Betty's replacement, Katie, showed up. We had loads of fun together. She showed me how to walk up and down stairs and get into and out of a car without dislocating my hip. But our relationship became short-lived when I engaged her in small talk about ice cream sundaes and hip rehabilitation.

Katie fired me for going to Friendly's for dinner with my wife. It turns out that insurance won't pay for home physical therapy visits if you go to Friendly's, even if it is the day before they close all their restaurants in Western New York, and even if you win two Friendly's network trivia games in a row (I think I made the five-year-old in the next booth cry when he didn't win.)

Katie told me she could give me a prescription for a physical therapy facility, but my wife won't let me go anywhere they have gym equipment because, um, I can't be trusted around treadmills, stationary bikes, and parallel high bars. Also, she doesn't like that all the elderly female hip replacement patients at these places keep asking me to dance (it was Weight Watchers all over again!) Plus, they don't play the Bee Gees or Abba at those gyms so what's the point?

But I digress.

Just three weeks after a total hip replacement and I am driving now, mostly in a straight line. You may want to avoid my neighborhood for a while.

I'm walking too. I alternate walking with a cane and a walker. My walker looks like a birdcage on wheels. Sometimes in public and within earshot of strangers I tell my wife that if she comes closer, I will push my walker to the side and give her a hug. I don't think she appreciates this. She tells me that there was nothing in our wedding vows about hugging a guy who uses a walker. I think she is mistaken about this, but I can't find our wedding video to prove my point.

I installed bumpers on my walker, which I made with inflatable green and blue doodles I stole from my neighbor's swimming pool. I only use my walker in the produce department at Wegmans, where I've organized a bumper-walker league. We meet every Tuesday morning at 10 a.m. near the asparagus. It is great fun. The goal is to see who can get to dairy and back first, via the deli and bakery. It is sort of like geriatric Pac-Man on wheels, with zucchini, watermelons and cantaloupes flying all over the place. There is a disco ball, live music, and EMTs on standby. You really work up a sweat. After the race we all hobble over to the food court where prizes are awarded by the assistant store manager.

The truth is that I don't use my walker anymore except for the Wegmans league, and I don't really need my cane. Sometimes I start hobbling along with my cane in a parking lot and then abruptly stop and start twirling it like a baton in a marching band. I toss it into the air, but not too high because I don't want them to take away my handicap parking tag, and then I catch it behind my back to show off.

I love my cane. It is hand carved of curly maple with double helical grooves along the staff. It is very stylish, and the ladies seem to like it. It gets me a seat quicker at restaurants too so I may use it a while longer.

Summer is just around the corner. I can't wait to try out my new hip. I'm shopping for an electric bicycle. I'm going to ride it by Betty's house and wave. I may even pop a wheelie!

Those Eight Awful Words

It's a funny thing about surgery. The pre-op instructions go on for pages and the post-op instructions even longer.

Some of the pre-op instructions are downright scary.

General stuff we say to scare you:

"You might get infected."

"You might scare your dog."

"Your head might fall off your body and roll around on the operating room floor until we can find it."

"You might bleed."

"We might replace your nose by mistake."

But I was fine with all that. I had a great surgical team who had taken all the precautions.

A few weeks before your surgery:

"Minimize your alcoholic intake to no more than one drink per day if you are pregnant, and no more than two drinks per day if you are a man or not pregnant." (I immediately increased my alcohol consumption to two White Russians per day instead of my usual one per week just to be safe.)

A day before your surgery:

"You may be asked to take a shower with a special germ-killing soap."

The day of your surgery:

"You may be asked to take another shower or two with a special germ-killing soap. If your wife sends us photos and you don't look clean to us, we may send over a contractor with a power washer or a fire hose to give you a thorough dousing."

Upon arrival at the hospital:

"You had better know your name and your birthday because the entire success of the operation depends on it. If you forget your name or your birthday or why you are visiting us at the hospital, we reserve the right to replace one or more body parts of our choosing.

We suggest you bring a friend or family member who can assist you in answering basic questions like your name and birthday in case you forget because even patients who scored a ninety-eight on the Iowa Tests of Basic Skills in fourth grade surprisingly forget who they are and when they were born on the day of surgery."

Shortly after arrival:

"We will make you wear compression socks. These help to reduce blood clots, but they won't likely match any suits, sport coats or slacks currently in your wardrobe.

An IV MAY be inserted into one of your veins" (you think?)

"In the operating room, you MAY be given one or

more of the following" (you think?):

"1. A medicine to help you relax (a sedative);

2. A medicine to numb the area (a local anesthetic);

3. A medicine to make you fall asleep (general anesthesia);

4. A medicine to make you love your mother-in-law.

If you persist in telling stories, telling us how to do the surgery or asking us questions that we don't know the answers to, we may skip directly to step 3 above.

Shortly after you are asleep:

We will review our notes and mark your body with permanent markers that remind us as to which body parts we are supposed to work on. Please don't be concerned if you find completed Tic-Tac-Toe games on your torso after you return home."

I was good with all that too. But I wasn't fine at all with the first eight words on the pre-op instructions. It's the first thing they warn you about:

"Nothing to eat or drink starting at midnight."

And then it happened …

At precisely 11 p.m. on Wednesday, May 5, it occurred to me that I wouldn't be able to eat anything except maybe ice chips and hospital food for days. I worried that I might never be able to eat again – ever! So I got into my car and drove, and drove …

11:05 p.m. "May I help you?"

"One soft-shell Mighty taco with beef, hot sauce and guacamole and an apple empanada please!"

11:15 p.m. "May I help you?"

"One single order Duffs wings, medium, extra crispy, side of bleu cheese, carrots and celery please."

And this from the Amherst Bee:

11:30 p.m. – A Wegman's customer and surgical pre-op patient following instructions was seen at the self-checkout scanner at the Sheridan Drive store, wearing a bathrobe, stuffing a half gallon of Breyer's French Vanilla ice cream, Hershey's chocolate syrup, a few bananas, and a jar of maraschino cherries into a paper bag. Several other elderly males – all soon to be patients at local hospitals themselves, all carrying the same pre-op instructions, were observed at adjacent scanners. One guy wearing bath slippers bought Milk Duds. Another guy bought peanut butter and jelly. Knowing winks and nods were exchanged.

To ensure a successful surgical outcome it has been my experience that you have to follow these instructions exactly. If you pop that last cherry into your mouth a minute past midnight you are asking for trouble.

Smile, laugh, love, and enjoy a banana split, but not a minute past midnight, or you are asking for trouble!

High School Reunions

Our 50th high school reunion is only a few months away. I can't wait! It officially starts on July 19th, but I started preparing well before that. I started taking One-A-Day vitamins on New Year's Day. The day after Memorial Day I'll go on a diet and maybe I'll even drive by a gym once or twice. On second thought, maybe I'll start my diet on Flag Day because I really look forward to Dairy Queen opening in early June. Oh heck, who am I kidding. I really enjoy hot dogs on the 4th of July too. So maybe I'll just wear a new suit instead of dieting. I do want to look my very best for all those beautiful girls who I was too afraid to ask for a date in high school.

High school reunions are interesting. When you first graduate from high school, you instantly recognize the faces of all 596 kids in your class, and you know about half of them by name.

At your 10-year reunion you can still recognize many of the faces, but you only remember half of the names you used to know.

At your 20-year reunion you still recognize your close

friends but even a complete review of your yearbook the day before won't help you recognize the people you sat next to in English class.

At your 30-year reunion you notice everyone whispering in each other's ears, and they are all saying the same thing, "Help me out here – who is that guy standing next to the punch bowl." (It's pretty embarrassing when you hear the response, "Kathy Wade - that's your husband!")

At your 40-year reunion, the organizers come to the rescue – they painstakingly scan the entire yearbook and make custom photo name tags for everyone, showing how you used to look forty years earlier and, to be helpful, they include your name in a nine point Arial Bold font. While the organizers meant well, I couldn't help but notice that most of the beautiful ladies in our class pinned their name tags to their dresses – in the exact location where they would pin a corsage for the senior prom. Um, I shouldn't probably say this out loud, but a lot of us old nearsighted guys were facing a dilemma that evening. I myself spent entirely too much time at our last reunion squinting at the name tags of my female classmates and going back and forth between the person's face and the breast-mounted photo until one lady just punched me.

It could be just me, but I think that there are a whole bunch of professional "reunion crashers" that start infiltrating these get-togethers around about the 40-year mark. I think they come for the food and drinks. They know we won't recognize them or turn them away and they bring fake IDs anyway. We only had 596 students in our graduating class, but I counted 800 people at our 45th reunion. I had very personal conversations with many of them who claimed they knew me, but I had absolutely no idea who they were. Some of them didn't even speak English. OK, maybe there weren't 800 people, maybe I talked to the same person two or three times during the evening, interrupted by cocktails, and just got confused.

I've noticed that our reunion committee has started scheduling our reunions every five years now, instead of every ten. They have informed me that when we get to the 55th reunion they are going to start scheduling them annually, and at our 60th anniversary, we are going to start meeting weekly. I'm not sure what all this means, but I have an appointment with an actuary to find out.

There is a lot of pressure with high school reunions, especially if you won one of those "Senior Most" awards in high school. At our last reunion the fellow who was voted "most talkative" was holding court at the bar with the "most humorous," interrupted only when the homecoming king and queen entered hand in hand with a drumroll. I wore shorts to my last reunion, on account of I was voted the "Best Legs in the Senior Class" and felt compelled to show off.

Those Senior Most awards are a blessing and a curse.

I was also voted "Most Likely to Succeed" (probably on account of my legs.) It made me proud at the time but I admit that I've spent the last fifty years wondering if I've succeeded or if I'd let my classmates down. I asked my wife if she thought I had lead a successful life so far. "Sweetie," she said, "you found true love and made true friends, we've raised a beautiful daughter, and we've helped a lot of people. So, don't be silly. Of course you've succeeded." She is right, of course; it's not about money, houses or cars – it's about family, friends, love and serving others.

I've talked to the organizers for our 50th reunion and even attended a planning meeting. It is so comforting to know that this year we are all going to wear sandwich boards, with 16" x 18" graduation headshots front and back, and our names in bold 128 point Times New Roman font. I'll be at the bar, sipping a Tanqueray and tonic, if you want to say hi and help me remember what high school we graduated from in 1974. Don't worry if you don't remember me or know my name – I probably won't remember your name either. I'll start every conversation with, "Hi, I'm Bob!" and you reply with, "Hi, I'm (fill in the blank)" and we'll get along just fine.

Those were the days my friend, we thought they'd never end.

Funerals, Gardenias, and the Coffee Urinal

I dislike the smell of lilies – I think because they remind me so much of funerals! I'm pretty sure that lilies are the main reason that families decline flowers at funerals.

I want to go on record in saying that you can send as many flowers to my funeral as you want, as long as they are gardenias. Or dandelions! I love the smell of gardenias and would love to take some of them with me to the great beyond. And I love dandelions too, because they remind me of my mom and that baseball season is upon us.

Many people don't know it, but florists discerned the true meaning of every flower from a stone tablet that Moses carried down from Mount Sinai long ago. The tablet has been missing for quite some time, but Indiana Jones is working on finding it. Here is basically what it said about lilies …

"Lilies represent the restored innocence of the soul of the departed." If this is true, then I prefer to be buried with a guilty soul and a pocketful of gardenias. They just smell better. If you want me to stay dead, then by all means pack me up with a bunch of lilies. If you loved me, or even just liked me, please leave your lilies in the ground, and bring me some gardenias.

Roses are popular at funerals too. Each color rose has a different meaning. White roses are the ultimate symbol of spirituality, purity, and innocence, while the classic deep red rose evokes love and grief. Yellow roses are given by friends of the decedent to show a deep bond. They are also given by guys who were turned down for the senior prom by the decedent. Rare pink roses are a way of saying thank you to the deceased person, not for dying, but for living. Pink roses with yellow stars signify that you spent entirely too much time during your lifetime inserting emoticons into your Facebook posts.

Sadly, you don't see many dandelions on display in funeral homes. It's not because they are not a pretty shade of yellow and represent wild and uncontrollable growth. It's because of a footnote on the back side of Moses' tablet that said that dandelions send a message that you considered the deceased person to be a weed.

When I was a young boy, I hated accompanying my parents to a funeral home for a wake. This awkward feeling persisted into adulthood. You just don't know what to say! It doesn't help that you stand in a long line to greet the grieving family, giving you and everyone else way too much time to secretly rehearse in your head the words you want to say.

When you finally get to the front of the line and are about to speak, your gracious host beats you to it with, "Thank you for coming," and you automatically say, "You're welcome," and then immediately forget everything you had rehearsed.

It is not until you get much older that you come to realize that you really don't have to say anything at all. Just a hug will do. That says everything words never could. And if you have to speak, just say, "I love you."

Sure, there are some things you should never say at a wake. You shouldn't mention that the decedent still owes you money, for example. And you shouldn't use the occasion to try out new vocabulary words. Just ask my late Aunt Flossie, my godmother and a master of the English language malaprop. When one of my uncles passed away and our Irish-Catholic family was gathered in the family room of the decedent, she yelled out from the kitchen to her dear husband, "Frank, come into the kitchen and I'll pour you a fresh cup of coffee from the urinal!"

Upon hearing my aunt's invitation, twelve of my aunts, uncles and cousins spit out their Irish whiskey simultaneously, and no one touched the coffee urn for the rest of the afternoon. My poor Uncle Ernie never enjoyed a cup of coffee again for the rest of his days. He just couldn't get the image out of his head!

It was an understandable *faux pas*. It wasn't that my

godmother was a sesquipedalian. Aunt Flossie had just never seen a 45-cup coffee urn before. All she had seen until then was an 8-cup Mr. Coffee carafe. She didn't specify what kind of urinal it was either. We were all left wondering whether it was a stand-up model or a sit-down model.

If you should outlive me and want to come to my funeral, I want you to be comfortable in knowing that there won't be any lilies in the funeral home or at the church. There won't be any coffee urinals either.

I would be honored to be the first person in the history of the world to have dandelions on display. And you don't have to worry about what to say to my surviving family. I'll give you the perfect words right here and now ...

"I love you. Smile, laugh, love, and remember!"

Christmas with COVID

The tree was up, the ornaments hung, the tinsel glistening. The fire was roaring, the puppies were sleeping, and baby Jesus was smiling from the family's manger. I cooked all day, and the Beef Wellingtons were wrapped and in the fridge. Haricot verts and winter black truffle potatoes were in the cooler, ready for the road trip to New Jersey. My wife and mother-in-law were already there – driving together with all the presents. I hung back with my daughter so she could attend a wedding. We would drive together on Christmas Eve morning.

And then it happened …

My daughter tested positive. And all that that entails. Off to quarantine she went while dad bought enough groceries to last her a month. "Take one of the Wellingtons!" I said as she headed for her car. "I will bring you the Port wine sauce!" I believe you should starve a cold and feed a virus with Beef Wellington and Port wine sauce.

And so it was, Christmas 2021. Alone with the puppies. They were happy. They eyed the second Wellington. "We could help you with that, you know!" We said a prayer in front of the manger. We knew Jesus would hear our prayer. We prayed for my daughter. We prayed for everyone affected by this virus.

And so it would be, alone with the puppies for Christmas. I made a chess move online. It was the silliest thing. I was playing against Marco, my next-door neighbor. We each made a move every fourteen days. It wasn't a very serious game. I told him my plans and he told me his. We chatted online during the game. We could just walk over to each other's house to make our moves in person. But we didn't. I sent him a text to let him know that he didn't have to watch our house over Christmas. I would be home after all. He is a chess player. He put it all together instantly.

"No man – you will not be alone for Christmas! You are coming here for dinner tonight!"

All the dinner guests took Covid tests on Christmas Eve. We all tested negative. I only knew Marco and Laurianne. But their family made me feel like family. Good people do that. It was magical! The house was a home filled with Christmas love. Lauri is a sweetheart. She is a mom to a large family of rescue cats and birds. And Marco is a gifted Spanish chef. He served a seven-pound beef tenderloin alongside my Wellington. He improved my dish – great chefs do that! He served egg and Spanish ham croquettes. I had never before enjoyed these Bechamel delights. If you ever get the chance – don't miss it!

We said grace. We drank wine. We dined. We told stories. We celebrated.

And then it occurred to me …

I was not alone. We are not alone. Merry Christmas!

(I love my neighbors, but I'm still planning a Queenside attack!)

Christmas Joy

When I was a young boy, I found great joy in seeing all the presents under the Christmas tree on Christmas morning, gathering all the ones with my name on them, and opening them all as fast as

I could.

Now that I am an old man, I find great joy in watching my loved ones open the presents I bought and wrapped just for them.

And then it happened ...

I'm not sure when it was, exactly, that I grew up. But I am glad I did.

Life Senior Member

I am so excited! I just received a letter in the mail from the IEEE (Institute of Electrical and Electronics Engineers). It brought me to tears, so I just had to share it with my wife …

"Sweetie – I just received this letter in the mail from the IEEE!"

"That's nice dear. What is the IEEE!"

"It's the Institute of Electrical and Electronics Engineers."

"That's nice dear. Do they want money?"

"No sweetie – they wrote to congratulate me!"

"For lifetime Best Buy purchases?"

"No silly. They selected me for IEEE Life Membership. They said I was truly distinguished, made lasting contributions to technology and made a significant impact on the growth of the IEEE!"

"You haven't been an engineer since 1984."

"I know, but they told me I'm now in the 'top echelon' of IEEE members."

"Do they know you call our contractor to change a

light bulb?"

"They didn't mention it, but they told me that my base membership dues are henceforth waived!"

"Honey – they think you are so old that you are retired and can't afford to pay your dues anymore."

"They even sent me a gold Life Senior Member card!"

"It looks an awful lot like an AARP Member card."

"They thanked me for my leadership, volunteerism and dedication to advancing technology for humanity!"

"I think the dogs are hungry."

"They thanked me for exemplary service."

"You need to bring in the trash cans from the street too."

"And here is the best part – they sent me a certificate – suitable for framing!"

"That's nice dear – you are not going to frame it are you?"

"Well, they did go through the trouble of printing it on card stock with a color printer!"

"Do you remember the last certificate you framed?"

"Not really."

"It was your certificate for 'Best Legs in the Senior Class of 1974'. It was signed by somebody named Mr. Falvo."

"Oh yeah, I remember. I walked on stage at the school with Sandy Fratello. She was voted 'Best Legs' for the girls."

"It's been sitting on a shelf in your closet for forty-seven years."

"Are you proud of me?"

"Yes dear, I am proud of you. Now why don't you put that new certificate in your closet with all the rest of them."

"Yes dear."

(All kidding aside, I am very proud to be an electrical engineer and the IEEE is a great group. By the way, engineering school was ten times harder than law school!)

Reflections and Do-Overs

I don't believe anyone who says they have no regrets. I believe we were made with a natural curiosity to look back now and then and at least wonder what, if anything, we would have done differently. I think it can be fun. I know it is for me. And so, in no particular order …

I would not have run a post-pattern and run into that maple tree in our front yard and chipped my two front teeth in junior high school in a touch football game when my little brother told me to "go long".

I would not have waited so long to have crowns made for my two front teeth.

I would not have quickly imbibed a glass of orange juice laced with vodka before giving a speech on stage in eighth grade when running for student council president, even though my campaign manager, recommended, mixed, and handed it to me to calm my nerves.

I would not have "hopped" as many cars as I did in the wintertime, or at least not have hopped them on Hyde Park Boulevard when I was twelve. That was really stupid.

I would not have stuck a stainless-steel fork in an electrical outlet to see what would happen when I was twelve.

I would not have stuffed as many firecrackers into the handlebars of my Sting-Ray bicycle and smuggled them across the Rainbow Bridge from Canada on that July 3rd summer day, also when I was twelve.

I would not have taken as many tomatoes from Mrs. Miller's garden when I slept out on my front porch with Gary McLaughlin, also when I was twelve. Mrs. Miller had a big family, and she made her own sauce. I think she needed those tomatoes more than I did. I didn't even like tomatoes when I was twelve.

I would not have done as many cannonballs off the low board at the Big Pool to splash the Wade sisters who were laying on their towels and trying to get a tan, also when I was twelve.

I would have done swan dives off the high board instead of cannonballs off the low board to try and impress the Wade sisters when I was twelve.

I would have stayed in my house and worked on my stamp collection more when I was twelve.

I would not have planted a hidden microphone in our basement when I was thirteen.

I would not have told my sister Mary that I heard her tell her boyfriend that she loved him on my hidden microphone in the basement when she was sixteen and

I was thirteen.

I would not have told my sister through an amplifier that everyone in our house could hear her tell her boyfriend that she loved him in the basement.

I would have run a lot faster out the front door of our house and down Niagara Avenue when my sister started chasing me with a twelve-inch cast iron frying pan in her hand right after I told her that I heard her tell her boyfriend that she loved him in our basement.

I would have told my sister Mary that I loved her and that I was sorry I listened to her private conversation with her boyfriend.

I would not have stolen that flashing round yellow barricade light on Robbins Drive in Hyde Park with Louie Zaninovich when I was fourteen so I could take it apart and find out how the circuit worked (it was a simple NPN bipolar transistor switching circuit).

I would not have made Louie hide that flashing yellow barricade light under his jacket as we carried it down Hyde Park Boulevard in the middle of the night. You could still see the flashing yellow light a mile away from under his jacket and if one of us was going to get arrested it was going to be Louie because I could run faster than he could, and he was carrying the heavy part of the barricade.

I would have brought a crosscut saw so that we could have cut the ends off of the six feet long piece of wood with the flashing yellow barricade light mounted in the center to make it easier for Louie and me to carry down Hyde Park Boulevard in the middle of the night.

I would not have made a peace sign with black electrical tape on that flashing yellow barricade light and hung it on my bedroom wall.

I would not have lied to my mom and told her that I bought that flashing yellow barricade light at a garage sale with my paper route money for a science project at school. (I don't think she believed me because she looked at me kind of funny.)

I would have turned off that flashing yellow barricade light at night so I could sleep better and get better grades. (My bedroom looked like a road construction site for a whole year – those batteries last a long time!)

I would have danced at junior high school dances, even though mostly only the girls were on the dance floor.

I would have asked a girl to dance with me at junior high school dances.

I would have gone to church more.

I would not have enjoyed as much Mogen David wine with Mark Aiduk and the priests when we were both altar boys and about to ring the bell and start the processional at the 11 a.m. Mass at Sacred Heart Church.

Scratch that last one. I would definitely do that one again exactly as it happened.

I would have played defensive back instead of wide

receiver on the varsity football team when Coach Scaletta asked me to.

I would have played baseball instead of run track in high school.

I would have learned how to play a musical instrument.

I would have tried harder to learn the French language.

I would have learned American Sign Language when I lived in the dormitory for the National Technical Institute for the Deaf in college.

I would not have given my hearing-impaired roommate a 150-watt stereo amplifier when I lived in the dormitory at the National Technical Institute for the Deaf in college.

I would have learned how to say, "Could you please turn the volume down," In American Sign Language when I lived in the dormitory at the National Technical Institute of the Deaf in college.

I would have taken advanced English composition classes in college when my professor waived me out of my freshman English class for writing the best essay she had ever seen in all her years of teaching instead of drinking Budweiser beer and playing ping pong with my floor mates.

I would have written more stories.

I would have written more thank-you notes to my

276 Robert P. Simpson

teachers and coaches.

I would have called that one girl I dated in college and told her why I wasn't going to call her anymore instead of just not calling her anymore.

I would have told that one girl that I stopped calling that I was afraid to keep dating her because I wasn't comfortable dating someone who jumped out of perfectly good airplanes every weekend and that I was afraid that her parachute wouldn't open and we would have to cancel our dinner reservation.

I would have said, "I love you" to my best friend the last time I saw him in the hospital, although I think he knew it.

I would have taken more bike rides and played more chess.

I would have seen Les Misérables on Broadway.

I would have gone to at least one of the Bills' four Super Bowls.

I would have bought an 8-cylinder Camaro instead of a 6-cylinder Camaro with my first paychecks after college.

I would have asked that beautiful woman that I ended up marrying for her phone number on the first evening that we met instead of being too afraid that she wouldn't give it to me and then spending days trying to find her number.

I would have never said, "I've got to go now mom,"

on the phone and would have listened for as long as she wanted to talk to me whenever she called.

I would have watched more Yankees games with my dad at his apartment after my mom was in heaven instead of just calling him on the phone after every home run.

But there are some things I would never change ...

I would have married the same beautiful woman, loved and raised the same beautiful daughter, adopted and loved the same Sheltie puppies, kept the same wonderful friends, taught the same courses, served the same clients, and told the same old stories whether people listened to them or not!

Calling it a Day

I knew the day would come, but somehow, I wished it wouldn't. I loved every minute in the classroom. I loved the questions. I loved the answers. I loved the lectures. I loved the banter and the debate. Mostly I loved the looks in their eyes and the smiles on their faces when I knew we had connected. I loved watching them sprout like flowers in front of my eyes.

I loved telling them stories about what it was like outside the classroom in the "real world." I knew my stories were old-fashioned like me, and they knew it too, but still they listened. I tried my best to pay forward what my wonderful teachers had given to me.

I thought a lot about my own teachers that last semester. I thought about Mrs. Brown, Miss Smith and Mrs. Dickerson at Hyde Park Elementary. I thought about Mr. Welch, Mr. Brick and Mr. Rizzo at Gaskill Junior High. I thought about Mr. Patti, Mr. Layman, Dr. Rohrkaste and Mr. Gomez at Niagara Falls High. I thought about Professors Frank Bogacki and Ralph Harper at R.I.T. and Tom Headrick at U.B. Law School.

I thought about Roger Stone who gave me a chance to teach at Hilbert College, Shubha Ghosh who gave me a chance at U.B. Law School, and Margaret Phillips who gave me a chance at Daemen College.

But mostly, I thought about my students – how smart they were, how inquisitive they were and how serious they were about learning. Boy, were they smart! I wonder if they ever knew that I learned way more from them than they learned from me!

It was fifteen beautiful years at the law school, ten years at Hilbert, and five years at Daemen. It takes a lot of time, effort, and money to prepare for and teach a higher education course, at least to do it right, but my wife encouraged me do it, because she loves me, and because she knew I loved teaching. She believed in paying it forward as much as I did.

I loved all my students, but two of them especially.

She didn't tell me she was enrolling in my patent law course. I was in New York City watching the world chess championship when I heard the news. And she brought along all her friends too. It was the largest class I ever taught. I had to ask the Dean if it was OK to teach my own daughter. He advised it could be a very good idea or a very bad idea. But alas, I am an optimist.

I remember what my daughter told me before the first class, "Dad – please remember that you are not to call on me in your class. And, if you feel the need to call on me, I am going to need to know both the question you are going to ask and the answer you expect me to give in advance!" She said it matter-of-factly with a sparkle in her eye. "That's nice sweetie, but that's NOT happening!"

We spent twenty-four classes together. For the first six classes, I received no feedback from her, none at all. So I asked my wife, "Is she enjoying the classes? I can't tell. Did she mention anything to you?" "Well dear, I do have a few text messages from our daughter. She sent some of them while sitting in your classroom. She said she is enjoying the course and learning a lot. She said you are a good teacher, but your stories are really corny and sort of boring. And she asked me to mention to you, should it ever come up in conversation, that you have a habit of tapping your right foot up and down on the floor for the first thirty minutes of every class when you are lecturing. She said, "It is SO ANNOYING!"

"Hmm – did she mention that I am really funny?"

"No dear – she didn't mention that."

"Hmm – did she mention that I am the best professor she has ever had in her life?"

"Gee dear – I'm afraid she didn't mention that either."

"She only mentioned my SO ANNOYING tapping right foot, didn't she?"

"I'm sorry dear."

I vividly remember entering the classroom the very next day after receiving this critique. I brought duct tape with me. I thought about taping my right foot to the floor. But I ended up just holding my knee with my hand during my opening lecture. It was awkward but I hoped it wasn't SO ANNOYING.

Teaching your daughter in a law school course seems like such a good idea at the beginning of the semester, much like joining a bowling league in Buffalo in September seems like a good idea, until you realize you will still be bowling in June. It hit me the day before our final exam, as I watched my daughter study for my final exam in the family room. Mom was quizzing her. I remained silent and neutral. It was excruciating to watch. That's when it struck me, if she didn't score an "A" on my exam I would have to hear about it for the rest of my life! She didn't let me down. She earned an "A" - and the grading was anonymous!

My second favorite student was a young man named Andrew McLaughlin, a student who followed me to my car after class one day. It was an 8 a.m. class. These were bright, serious students in their second and third year of law school. We met in the basement classroom – deep in the bowels of O'Brian Hall. There were about twenty students in my class that semester. A few wanted to become patent lawyers. Some just wanted to know something about intellectual property law. Others took the course because it fit their schedule. They were all a bit groggy first thing in the morning, dressed in typical

282 Robert P. Simpson

student attire – jeans and casual shirts – sipping their first coffee of the day as I began my lecture.

About midway into the semester, on a warm April morning as class ended and students came to see me with questions about the material, Andrew approached me first. Within earshot of his classmates, he just came right out and asked me, "Would you happen to have a job for a law clerk?" His classmates gasped. This was not how you applied for a job in the legal profession!

"Let me answer your classmates' questions, Andrew, and then we can talk."

Andrew walked me to my car. He told me he had a degree in molecular biology and wanted to be a patent attorney. He told me he was hungry to learn and would even work for free just to get the experience. I told him that I had to get back to my office to take a call with an Examiner at the Patent Office. I invited him to join me there. I warned him that we didn't have an opening for a law clerk but that we could chat about the profession in general.

On the way to my office, I called my wife and told her one of my students was coming over for a visit. "You didn't offer him a job, did you?" She knew that I tend to take in law clerks like some people take in dogs and cats. "No – I warned him that we don't have any openings."

Andrew was late, thirty minutes late, not the best first impression for someone who wants a job. I wondered why.

And then it happened ...

Andrew walked through the glass doors wearing a pressed blue suit, white shirt, shiny black shoes, and a red tie to match his hair! He had gone home after class to change his clothes!

I had to take my phone call, so I left him with Ellen to chat. My call was lengthy. As the call ended, I received a text from Ellen, "DO NOT LET ANDREW LEAVE OUR OFFICE WITHOUT OFFERING HIM A JOB!" He had won her over in forty-five minutes! We hired him on the spot. We didn't have a need, but we hired him anyway.

He worked all summer for us. He was brilliant. He soaked it all in. He didn't always agree with what I was teaching him, and I could tell when he didn't. He would tilt his head slightly and ask me, respectfully, "Really?" "Really, Andrew!"

Sadly, Andrew was diagnosed with cancer during his third year of law school. Even sadder, with his background in molecular biology, he knew more about this terrible affliction than most. Somehow, even through radiation and chemotherapy, he managed to graduate and pass both the New York State and Patent Office bar exams. His cancer went into remission, and he joined our firm as an associate a month after taking the New York bar exam.

He did magnificent work. He was one of those rare lawyers who could do both patent and trademark work.

He wrote beautifully. He wrote patent applications on complicated stuff in the morning and then switched gears and wrote trademark briefs in the afternoon. And he was a joy in the office. Our clients loved him. Everyone loved Andrew.

And then it happened, again …

The cancer returned, with a vengeance. He juggled work with cancer treatments while taking care of a newborn baby. He missed quite a bit of work. But our whole firm came together for Andrew. We all took a piece of his workload and did his work for him so we could pay him through the treatments.

I saved our last text messages on my phone for many years after Andrew left this world.

"You did a fantastic job Andrew. Our clients love you, and so do we. I am so glad you came to ask me for a job after our class that morning in April. And you achieved your dream of becoming a patent lawyer."

"And I think I was just starting to get good at it?"

"Yes, Andrew, you were more than good, you were great at it!"

"Really?"

"Yes, Andrew, really!"

It was, of course, tragic that Andrew left this world way too soon, but I take some small comfort in knowing that he achieved a few of his important life goals, served others and left an impressive body of legal writing for us to admire and learn from. And he gave us all the honor of watching him do it. "Yes, Andrew, you made a difference!"

Andrew and Adelina made it all worthwhile. All my students did. I hope they all learned as much from me as I did from them.

Sadly, it is time to call it a day. It is time to blow out the candle and make room for others to carry the flame.

European Delivery and My Bavarian Friend

As we raced down the Autobahn at 140 mph, I remember having only two thoughts: "How lucky I am to be in Germany with my new friend and client, Werner Reichert (pronounced 'Vierner');" and "I hope Werner is a good driver."

I really didn't know if we were in Germany – my eyes were closed! But Werner didn't seem to mind. We talked about a lot of things, as if we had known each other forever. We talked about our work and our families. We talked about cooking. We talked about German beer. We talked about our moms, Blanche and Maria, who happened to share the same birthday of September 10. And we talked about cars. His was a beautiful black BMW 5 Series – the ultimate driving machine. He didn't know what I drove, until he asked, "BAWB (the Bavarian pronunciation of 'Bob'), what kind of car do you drive?"

Well, Werner, I drive a green, 1998 GMC Safari minivan!" I replied sheepishly.

"What is a Safari?"

"Well, it's big and green and long and slow. It can seat my daughter and five of her friends and our dog, and I can even sleep in it if I need to."

He was not impressed.

"BAWB – you must get a new car! You cannot do my company's patent work and drive a minivan. (Dr. Reichert is a German and European Patent Attorney.) It is embarrassing. You MUST drive a German car!"

"Will you tell that to my wife?"

"Yah-yah!" (This is Werner's favorite phrase.)

"What kind of car should I buy?"

"Mercedes Benz."

"No Werner, that is too ostentatious. I cannot drive a Mercedes Benz."

"Volkswagen."

"No Werner, I cannot not drive a Beetle or a bus. I am not cool enough to drive a Volkswagen."

"Audi."

"Maybe. What else?"

"BMW. It is the ultimate driving machine."

I admired Werner. He loved his car. I wanted to be like him, and so I replied, "Ok, Werner, when I get home I will trade in my minivan and buy a BMW."

"Yah-yah!"

A week after my return home, I received an email from my friend, "BAWB, have you bought a BMW yet?"

"No, Werner, but I made an appointment to visit the dealership next Saturday at 10 a.m."

"Gut – I vill be there!" (Translation – "Good, I will be there.")

I thought he was joking. But, to my great surprise, he booked a flight from Munich to Buffalo. He flew over the Atlantic Ocean to help me buy a car. Who does that? He rented a car and drove himself to a hotel.

I arrived at the dealership at 9:45 a.m. I waited for my sales representative, Rich, to meet me.

And then it happened …

At precisely 10 a.m. that Saturday morning, Rich appeared, accompanied by my friend Werner. Rich had a contract in hand.

"Are you ready to meet, Rich?" I asked.

"There is no need, Bob. Your friend, Werner, has already negotiated your deal. He arrived a half hour ago. He got you the best deal you could hope for. He is Bavarian, you know. And he knows cars!"

Werner negotiated a lease on a BMW 750LI and arranged to have it delivered to Freising, Germany.

"BAWB – I saved you a lot of money. You vill use the savings to come to Germany to pick up your car. You vill bring your wife, your daughter, your brother-in-law and your mother-in-law. We vill drink beer and enjoy apple strudel. And I vill show you how to drive your car."

And so it happened ...

Werner met us at our hotel in Munich. He wore Bavarian lederhosen. He drove us to the BMW factory where we were treated like royalty. We sipped cappuccino and enjoyed warm German pastries. The salesmen were dressed impeccably. They conversed with Werner in German and with my family in perfect English. Werner checked out my car to make sure it was perfect.

And then we drove ...

We drove on the Autobahn. I drove at eighty mph. I thought I was cool. And then Werner told me to take the next exit and pull over.

"BAWB – you have a BMW 7 Series. You are driving too slow! You must drive in the passing lane. Only BMW 5s and 3s drive in the slow lane. Let me show you!"

We drove at 100 to 140 mph. He seemed so relaxed for someone driving so fast. We drove from Munich to Hofkirchen, Werner's hometown, a beautiful Bavarian village. We met his mom, Maria, and sister, Marlies, and brother-in-law, Helmut. We enjoyed a beautiful outdoor summer party at the home of Werner's architect, serenaded by a string quartet. Werner's talented and beautiful girlfriend, Sabine, now his wife, played in the quartet. Ellen played the piano and sang a few songs for our German friends. We didn't speak the same language but it didn't seem to matter, they made us feel like family. German wine calmed my excitement from the Autobahn.

Werner drove my new car around Germany for a week after we left. We visited Venice, Florence, Pisa, Rome and Sicily while he sped around the Autobahn. As we departed for home, Werner dropped my car off in Frankfurt where it eventually found its way to an ocean liner headed for America. It arrived with German license plates still in place. I kept those plates on display in my office for years. And I drove BMWs for a dozen years after that. Truth be told, I rarely drove them faster than sixty-five mph. I never told Werner how slow I drove. But I think he knew. I think he knew that's why I traded in my BMW for an Audi and he knows that I'm still not cool enough to drive a Volkswagen.

Werner and Sabine have their own law firm in Regensburg now. They have a beautiful daughter, Serafina, too. We send each other as much work as we can. We've visited with our Bavarian friends many times in the U.S. and Germany since that first visit twenty years ago. He even made a surprise visit to celebrate my fiftieth birthday, and his mom, Maria, even taught me how to make apple strudel. We still talk about work, family and cars, and, when we are together, I always ask him to drive. Yah-yah!

Dogs Are Like That
(I Can See Clearly Now)

It was a sunny summer day. Ellen and I were pitching a prospective client in Toronto. We were playing the game and chasing the dream. We were trying to help people protect their stuff.

I went first, explaining everything I knew about patents. I had done this hundreds of times. It is my passion. I love doing this. I love helping inventors protect their inventions.

I was just getting started when the clock struck noon. I could see that their brain sponges were full. We broke for lunch at an outdoor Mediterranean bistro. I remember the taste of Limonana - Israeli lemonade flavored with muddled mint. I can still see and taste it in my mind's eye. I can still see the vibrant green mint and the bright yellow lemons. I remember wondering how I could have lived this long and yet not know about this delightful beverage.

It was Ellen's turn after lunch. I sat back to listen to her explain trademark law as I had hundreds of times before. I loved listening to Ellen. She made it sound so easy and understandable. Few people know that trademark law is a lot more complicated than patent law. I could tell from the expression on the client's face that Ellen had won him over. I glanced at my watch. It was 2:52 p.m. on Thursday, August 6, 2009.

And then it happened …

The lights went out! Darkness filled the room. I could hear Ellen's sweet, calming voice but I couldn't see her. I wondered why she was continuing to talk in the dark. I wondered why no one mentioned the power failure. I glanced quickly to the ceiling as the lights dimmed. The last image I saw was of a fluorescent light overhead. It took a few seconds for it to register. But then it hit me. Fluorescent bulbs aren't dimmable. It wasn't a power failure. Something was terribly wrong. In the blink of an eye, I was blind!

I excused myself and stumbled to the restroom in the dark. Everything was cloudy. I was dizzy. I needed a mirror. I needed to figure out what was happening. I needed to be alone.

I covered my left eye with my hand and looked in the mirror. I could see my face and my face looked scared. I covered my right eye and it hit me again. I could see a sliver of light shaped like a slice of pie between twelve and two on a clock face, but the rest of the clock face was as black as the night sky. I bent over and washed my face in the sink, as if the cool water could restore my vision. I opened both eyes and looked in the mirror, but the image was wavy and distorted as my brain tried to make sense of its new signals. I sat down and cried.

I thought of Ellen back in the conference room trying to win this prospective client's trust. I thought about bursting into the room, announcing that I was blind, and asking that someone call an ambulance. But then it occurred to me. No client would hire a blind lawyer. So, I washed my face again and washed away my tears. I found my way back to the conference room and sat silently in the dark for fifteen agonizing minutes.

As Ellen finished and the meeting ended, I rose and extended my hand. I waited to see if the client would find my hand and shake it. I couldn't see him or his hand. But I could hear his voice and I nodded in his direction as he shook my hand.

I held my wife's arm as we left the building. The client was watching as I handed my car keys to Ellen. I asked her to drive my car. I remember her words to this day, "You know I hate driving your car, it's too big!"

"Please just drive it out of the parking lot," I pleaded.

"OK, but you are driving us home!"

When we turned the corner and were out of sight of the client, I removed my tie and wrapped it around my head, covering my eyes. I reclined the passenger seat and started to cry. It was then that Ellen knew there was something wrong. It was then I told her I was sorry, but I couldn't see, and I couldn't drive us home.

As we raced down the Queen Elizabeth Way at seventy miles an hour, with Ellen on the phone with the surgeon in Williamsville, I could hear him promise to wait for us at his office. It was a helpless feeling. I was filled with crazy thoughts. I wondered if I would ever practice law again. I wondered how long it would take for me to learn how to read Braille. I wondered if I would ever write any of the stories floating around in my head. I wondered why I couldn't see. I wondered if I would forevermore dress like a pirate wearing an eye patch. I was in no physical pain, but the emotional pain was overwhelming. You don't think about your eyesight every day. You take it for granted – until it's gone.

The doctor greeted us at the door. His office was empty except for us. He put me in a chair and peered into my left eye with bright lights. But I could not see them. Ellen sat nearby. I couldn't see her, but I sensed her fear. I heard the doctor say, "Oh my!" Then he stepped back and told us. I had suffered an 80% detachment of the retina in my left eye. "I'll schedule surgery as soon as possible. There is some good news here, the macula appears to be intact, but we have to act fast."

Friday was a dark day, lying in bed, both eyes closed, with our Sheltie, Sheena, by my side, listening to music, wondering, worrying and praying. The operating room was booked solid with other emergencies that day, so it wasn't until 6 a.m. on Saturday, two days after the detachment, that Ellen drove me to the hospital.

I remember little about the surgery, which took three hours under general anesthesia. The doctor used medical words like vitrectomy and scleral buckle. He told me he was going to reattach my retina with a laser, give me a new lens and inject new vitreous and gas into my eye. I told him I didn't care what he had to do – I would give him everything I owned, even my prized stamp collection, if he could restore my eyesight. As the surgery was coming to a close, I could hear the surgeon talking with his nurse about a vacation he had enjoyed in Puerto Rico. It sounded nice. He described a Margarita. I asked out loud, "Straight up or frozen?" I think I startled everyone in the O.R. I immediately regretted asking my question. It is not a good idea to startle the doctor who is trying to reattach your retina. They put me back to sleep.

When I awoke in recovery, the doctor told me the surgery was successful. He sent me home and told me to lie face down and not move for twenty-four hours. This is easier said than done. The gas inside my eye would rise toward the back of my eye and help the retina to reattach and heal. Ellen tuned the television to a PBS station as I laid prostrate on my bed with my head in a brace facing the floor. Sheena laid down beside me on the bed.

Ellen left the house to buy some groceries. I couldn't see the television, but I could hear it. It was a show about the Blind Association of Western New York, explaining their programs for the visually impaired. "Are you kidding me?" I reached for the remote to change the channel but couldn't find it. I gained an appreciation for the Blind Association and everything they do for the visually impaired.

I spent the next four months recuperating with a high-powered lens in my left eye. I don't know why my surgeon replaced my lens with a magnifying glass, but I could literally see the pores in my fingertips and every detail in the stamps of my collection. But I couldn't see anything farther than three inches away from my face. My head hurt when I tried to see out of my right eye, so I usually just kept my eyes closed. My dear friends Vic and Barry stopped by to check on me and cheer me up. Vic even drove me around town and challenged me to chess games when I couldn't see. True blue friends are like that – they stick with you when you are down.

Sheena never left my side after the surgery. She knew I wasn't well.

Dogs are like that.

She guided me to a lawn chair in the middle of our back yard every day. She sat under the chair in the shade. I drank lemonade and gave her watermelon treats. We listened to music, and I told her stories – stories in my head but not yet written. I promised her I would write them all down one day if I could. I know it seems silly to make a promise to a dog, but it didn't seem silly at the time.

I couldn't practice law for four months. I couldn't drive either. I was legally blind. Even though I could see out of my right eye, I couldn't read, and I couldn't write. My brain was confused, and I would get terrible headaches when I tried to read or write. My doctor advised me to not even try, so I usually kept both eyes closed. He explained that my brain was struggling to combine the signals from my good and bad eyes. For fifty-three years it was trained to combine one way, and it would be painful to retrain itself to use only one eye.

The semester started in September, but I couldn't teach. Ellen taught the trademark law part of my course. Later in the semester, the syllabus called for four classes on patent law. A colleague drove me to the college. I taught those four classes, three hours each, in the blind. I couldn't see my students, but I could hear them. One of them advanced my slides and read the first few words out loud. I taught them everything I knew from memory. Ellen graded their final exams. They all passed with flying colors.

On December 19, my surgeon removed my magnifying glass lens, which had absorbed all the gas in my eye and become cloudy and replaced it with a new

298 Robert P. Simpson

lens. The next day I anxiously removed the patch. After more than four long months of darkness, the first thing I saw was Ellen's beautiful smiling face. Then I looked down as Sheena barked. I smiled at her, and she barked again. She knew I could see her. She knew I was better.

Dogs are like that.

Like many nearsighted people, I had a 1 in 20,000 chance of suffering a detached retina. It runs in our family. My older sister and younger brother both suffered detached retinas too. I had an 86% chance of recovering my full vision after surgery. I had an excellent surgeon. I had the world's best wife cheering me on and I had man's best friend at my side. My vision is now 20/30 in my left eye.

We landed the client. I told him what happened. He had no problem hiring a blind lawyer.

Ten years after plunging into darkness, I finally wrote down all those stories I promised to Sheena in the summer of 2009. Sadly, she didn't live to see me write them. But she heard them all before anyone read them.

When you bring a dog into your family, you promise to take care of them for the rest of their life. You promise to feed them, give them fresh water, take care of them when they are sick, play with them and give them lots of love. They really don't ask for that much in return. My dog helped me through some very dark days – literally. When you make a promise, I think you should keep it,

even one made to your dog.

Smile, laugh, love, and remember!

I can see clearly now!

Afterword
(Text Messages from Mary)

July 25, 2018 12:37 p.m.

Hi Bob, So great to see you & Ellen at the baby shower for MaryBeth. Tell Ellen she looks as young and beautiful as ever. Let us know how Adeline and Adelina are doing. Love you all. 🖤🖤🖤

> Thanks Mary! Beautiful shower! Adelina is in day 2 of the New York bar exam.

October 21, 2018, 3:42 p.m.

Hi Mary – can you please send me your email address? I'd like to send you my stories.

> Sure.

October 22, 2018, 4:57 p.m.

Bob, are you writing a book? I missed a step. No doubt your stories are book worthy. Good for you!!! 🙂

☺☺☺☺☺ How did this come about? I'm so proud of you! ♥

Did you get my email with the stories?
Checking.

I wrote about 40 stories so far. My friends on Facebook seem to like them. A number of my friends asked me to consider publishing them in a book. My friend, Frank Mariani, is going to illustrate it. He is SO talented. We are going to donate profits to two charities, one for juvenile cancer research and one for spina bifada. Frank and his wife, Bonnie, lost a young daughter, Lindsay, to cancer. I'm going to do a storytelling event in Niagara Falls, sell some books and hopefully help some kids.

My friends ranked my stories. So far Bumblebees and Dandelions is number 1 on everyone's list, tied with Lost in Niagara Falls. I wrote the first one for mom and the second one for dad. There is another story in my head about my best friend, Danny, and our epic bicycle trip to Allegany. I have a good feeling about that story, but it will be painful to write.

Just read the rest of your text. Wonderful to donate to charity, especially spina bifada. Mom & Dad would be so proud of you. God bless your heart of gold.

♥The spina bifada donation is in memory of our dear sister, Kathleen Ann. I was only three when she left us but I picked all those dandelions to make mom smile again. Ironically, a dear high school friend named Kathy has a wheelchair-bound daughter who suffers from the same birth defect. They are the sweetest people you could ever hope to know – always suffering and smiling at the same time. I wrote Bumblebees for them too.

Wow, not even three months. She was a beautiful baby. They gave her a beautiful wake and funeral. You must have been around 3.

I was 3½.

I must have been 6. I remember her and how Mom was so protective of her ...

OK. Just started reading and you already have me in tears. This is going to take a full box of tissues. 🩶

October 22, 2018, 10:57 p.m.
Aww – remember to smile too!

October 23, 2018, 10:28 p.m.
Please let me know if you think they are good enough to publish. Be honest! Just found out Adelina passed the bar exam!

Great news Bob! So proud of her. Congratulate her for us! 👍

October 24, 2018, 1:11 p.m.
Bob, just read "Bumblebees & Dandelions". You truly

reflect a childlike innocence in your story. You brought me into your world and made me smile. Thank you. ☺

> Thank you, Mary. As an author of beautiful poetry yourself I'm sure you know it is hard to judge your own work. "Bumblebees" and "Lost in Niagara Falls" were the two that most of my friends rated as best. Let me know what you think about Lost in NF. Love, Bob

"Lost in Niagara Falls" had me laughing when you first got lost in the women's lingerie department at Kmart. It's a great story. Did you really walk all the way home from Falls St.? It's a great narrative. I love your style. ☺😎

> Thank you! Yes – really got lost in Kmart and really walked all the way home from Falls St. in 4th grade. Remember when you and I went hiking in the hills behind Uncle Ernie's cabin on Cotter Road in Ellicottville and got lost for hours and Dad called the State Police?

Sure I do! You were 12 and I was 15. I was very scared but you kept reassuring me that we would find our way back. But I could tell you were completely lost and as scared as me. I also remember the time I lost Mom & Dad in Slipko's. I was hanging on to someone else's shopping cart. I looked up and there was a stranger staring down at me. Yikes! Lost in Slipko's!! No worse panic for a little kid.

> How old were you? You should write a story about

it! Did you read Mike's story about gold mining in the back yard?

Young enough to panic! ☺ I would write but I don't have the gift for embellishment as you do. You add a lot of detail that makes me feel the memory as I read. Mike did a nice job on the gold mining story. You both bring your memories to life as you describe your thought process as you tell your story.

Embellishment? "Truth is one of our greatest resources. – let us economize it!" (Mark Twain)

You chose the perfect mentor. I'm sure you studied him. Do you remember our Green Lakes adventure? You and I were rowing a boat out in the middle of the lake (180 feet deep). Dad was slightly upset because we were all the way out in the middle and he wanted to pack us up and leave. I think it was the last, if only, family vacation we ever had. Fond memories.

I remember! I jumped off the diving board and into the lake on that trip, got a cramp in my leg underwater and almost drowned. I also met a cute girl from Manlius, NY named Becky Courtwright playing softball. I was 12 and she was 14. She sent me a Christmas card 6 months later! I thought we would get married but I didn't think mom and dad would let me ride my bike to Manlius to date her and I didn't even know where Manlius was. I knew when I was under water that I wouldn't marry Becky if I drowned that day.

So interesting how we all have different takes on the same event. Gloria met a boy named Dick Cantin, not surprising. I remember the tiny camper and sleeping out under the stars. I wonder what Mike remembers. If it wasn't for mom that vacation would never have happened. But I don't remember your diving incident. Not to ignore. That's scary stuff.

Yeah, I was about 8 feet underwater after the dive off the high board when the cramp hit. The water was dark and green and I became disoriented and couldn't kick my feet. I was scared to death. I remembered my Red Button swimming test and just held my breath for as long as I could and hoped I would float to the surface. I was just about to exhale and probably drown when I saw sunlight through the water so I flapped my arms like crazy. I never told anyone because I knew dad almost drowned in Lake Ontario because of a stomach cramp and I didn't want to upset mom and dad.

Close call.

[We exchanged many more text messages in October-November but many are protected by attorney-client privilege and can't be published. We visited each other at Patrick and MaryBeth's house in Niagara Falls at Thanksgiving. We missed each other at Christmas because we were in different cities. We exchanged texts about birthday gifts in March and April. I had my hip replaced in March, 2019 and Mary helped me through it. She helped me through my retina reattachment in 2009, my knee replacement in 2012, and my foot reconstruction surgery in December, 2019.]

March 16, 2019, 7:30 p.m.

Good luck with your surgery Tuesday, Bob. I'm praying for you. ♥ Will you ask Ellen to call me when you are out of recovery? Love you, Mary.

Thank you, Mary! Will do. I am so looking forward to this. The pain is unbearable. Love you too! ♥

March 19, 2019, 8:40 p.m.

(the day of my hip replacement surgery)

Glad to hear you are doing well. I'm looking forward to talking with you tomorrow. Thought you might want to get some rest first. Hope your recovery is fast and painless. ♥ Love you! Mary

Love you, Mary! ♥

March 25, 2019

Hi, I'm thinking of you and wondering how you're feeling. Do you have a physical therapist coming to the house? I hope you're making steady progress. One question, now that you're home recuperating, where do I send your mail? Just wondering. Love you, Mary. ♥

Still send mail to office. I am still in the witness protection program. No one knows where I live, not even me. In lots of pain now. Today was first day of PT. My therapist is a 6'5" Russian woman. I think she won a gold medal in weightlifting at the Olympics. She scares me. I ran away from defensive linemen who were smaller than her when I played football in high school. She beat me up from 1-2 p.m. By 3 p.m. I was crying. By 4 p.m. I was hugging my dogs. By 4:30 p.m. I was swallowing pain meds. By 5 p.m. I was writing a story about it.

Take the pain meds! Beginning therapy is the toughest part. I know how you feel. 🖤

I think I write better stories while on pain meds. I seem to write a lot of stories about surgeries while in la-la land. 🖤

March 29, 2019, 9:16 p.m.

Happy Birthday Bob, I hope you enjoyed your day. ☺ We had some dinner guests over who just left but you've been on my mind all week. I hope you are feeling better day by day. I'm with you all the way … Sending all my love, Mary 🖤

Tried to call you earlier but got voicemail. Just read your beautiful card. I enjoyed the chocolate-covered strawberries too! Love you! 🖤🖤

July 6, 2019, 8:50 p.m.

We are arriving Wed., going to the book launch Thurs. and heading home Fri. Do you think there will be extra books at the signing? We're looking forward to the big event. ☺ Love you, Mary

> Hard cover or paperback? Just let me know and I can set it aside for you. Safe travels! Love you! Bob

Hard cover please. Thanks Bob. 🖤

July 10, 2019, 6:54 p.m.

(One day before book launch)

On our way driving through Rochester. Saw FB post. Should we arrive before 5 with MaryBeth's Lindt's chocolates for refreshment table?

> 4:45 would be good.

Okie dokie. ☺

> 4:30 might be better. Just heard from friends – they are setting up cookie tables at 4:30.

OK.

July 14, 2019, 9:19 p.m.

Hi Mary – just a note to thank you and Al for traveling so far and attending the book launch. I hope you are now able to get some rest. Let me know what you think of the book when you get the chance. I feel like an actor after opening night waiting for the bad reviews to pour in! Love you, Bob

July 14, 2019, 9:44 p.m.

We wouldn't have missed it for the world. You are a natural, Bob. With love, Mary

July 16, 2019, 6:18 p.m.

Hi Mary – Thank you for that sweet card I received today. It meant the world to me that you and Al would drive so far for the event! Love you!

July 18, 2019, 9:20 p.m.

Bob, I'm really enjoying your book. I read a chapter or two each nite before bed. I find it relaxing and I love reading about those special times in your life. I love your style – and it does sound like you've been writing for years. Waiting on Volume Two! Love you. 🖤
[It was this message that inspired me to write a Volume Two, "And Then It Happened …" for Mary.]

Aww, it's funny you use the word "relaxing". I heard from another friend today who is also reading a couple of chapters a day and she also said it was, "insightful, funny and relaxing." The stories themselves were really effortless to write – about 15 minutes each – just writing what I hear in my head, except for "Top of the World" – that one took about two hours to write spread out over two weeks, not because I didn't hear the whole thing but because I kept breaking down and crying every other paragraph. We had great parents, Mary. We were very lucky! Love you!

[I had my right foot reconstructed through three surgeries on Dec. 3, 2019. Mary sent me a ton of text messages before and after the surgery. She came to Buffalo to visit her son, daughter-in-law, and granddaughter for Christmas. We were invited but I couldn't walk and even driving in a car as a passenger was too painful. She came to visit me instead on December 27. She didn't know where I lived so I had to give her my address. We always joked that I was in the witness protection program but the truth is that I just prefer to have my snail mail delivered to my office so very few people know where I live. I, myself, still use a GPS to drive the 2 miles from my office to my home.]

December 18, 2019, 2:24 p.m.
One thing though, I don't know where you live! 🙂

🙂 It's more fun that way! Mike and I didn't know where you lived when we came to visit you in Connecticut in 1976 but that didn't stop us!

December 27, 2019, 11:39
How are you feeling today, Mary?

Ok.. We're. Just. About to head over. Ok?

[I was concerned by her punctuation and terseness in this text. Her text messages were always so grammatically perfect – always better than mine.]

Sure. Come in through garage.

[We visited for a couple of hours two days after Christmas. We reminisced and she told me how much she loved her son, Patrick, and daughter-in-law, MaryBeth, and her new granddaughter, Aurora Mae. Our last words to each other were, "I love you," as we embraced. I am so happy my last words weren't, "Sure. Come in through garage."

Mary Louise Simpson Peret went to heaven on January 4, 2020 after a short bout with leukemia. She never told me she had leukemia. I'm not sure she knew herself. My doctor advised me against traveling to Connecticut for her funeral. Earlier in her life, my brother, Michael, donated a kidney to a stranger so Mary could move higher on the donor list and receive a life-saving kidney transplant herself. She received her kidney just 24 hours after Mike donated his. Her husband, Al, is a gem. That's the kind of loving family I have been blessed with, three beautiful sisters and a beautiful little brother, loving parents, and a beautiful wife and daughter. Mary was an angel on earth, loved by many. I am sure she is an angel in heaven. How could I not love her? How could I not dedicate my second book to her? My only regret is that I didn't finish it in time for her to read it. But sometimes, when I am alone, I read the stories out loud just for her. I know she is listening.

I still shed tears for Mary whenever I think of her. I

suspect I always will. I suspect everyone sheds tears for the loved ones they have lost. But don't run from those tears. Let them flow. Embrace them. Because those tears inevitably lead to smiles and those smiles lead to laughs. And smiles and laughs are two of the purest forms of love. So when I read my stories out loud to Mary, I know that she is not only listening. I know that she is smiling and laughing and remembering. And I know that she still loves me as I do her.

About the Author

Robert P. Simpson was born on Holy Thursday but it wore off. He is a patent attorney, college and law school professor, electrical engineer, mediocre chess player, and storyteller from Niagara Falls, New York. He graduated from Rochester Institute of Technology and State University of New York at Buffalo School of Law. He has practiced law for more than thirty-six years, written thousands of patent applications, and more than 150 short stories. He resides in Williamsville, New York with his wife, Ellen, and their Shelties, Missy, Mia, and Cocoa.

Milton Keynes UK
Ingram Content Group UK Ltd.
UKHW021128260224
438488UK00009B/50